JAINA BRONZES FROM HANSI

JAINA BRONZES FROM HANSI

DEVENDRA HANDA

INDIAN INSTITUTE OF ADVANCED STUDY
RASHTRAPATI NIVAS, SHIMLA - 171005

ARYAN BOOKS INTERNATIONAL
NEW DELHI

ISBN-81-7305-234-4

First Published 2002

Published by

INDIAN INSTITUTE OF ADVANCED STUDY
Rashtrapati Nivas, Shimla - 171 005

in association with

ARYAN BOOKS INTERNATIONAL
Pooja Apts., 4B, Ansari Road, Darya Ganj, New Delhi-110 002 (India)
Tel.: 3287589, 3255799; Fax : 91-11-3270385; E-mail : aryanbooks@vsnl.com

Computer Typeset at ABI Prints & Publishing Co., New Delhi
Printed in India at B.B.N. Printers, New Delhi

Foreword

The history of Bronze images going back to the Indus-Saraswati culture has a rich and variegated story. Unfortunately Haryana has remained *terra incognita* till quite recently from the point of view of Bronze images. The discovery of Bronze images from a hoard of Hansi has brought this region also on the map of Bronze images and culture.

The Hansi hoard has given 58 Bronze images belonging to the Śvetāmbar and Digambar sects of Jainism along with two Buddhist images. These images belong to the period from the 8th to 10th century A.D.

The present study of Hansi images reveals many interesting aspects of religious life of the region such as the harmony between Jainism and Buddhism, the popularity of Pārśvanāth followed by other tirthaṅkara, the discovery of first metallic image of Mallināth and the early examples of metallic images of Sarvatobhadrikās. The author has thrown light on the techniques of making these images. I felicitate Shri Devendra Handa for his very fascinating original contribution with religion and art history of almost unknown Hansi images through this monograph. I am sure the present monograph would add to the richness of libraries and would go a long way in situating many unanswered questions in the realm of art and history of Haryana against the broader perspective of Indian art and culture.

Shimla
May 14, 2002

V.C. Srivastava
Director

Preface

The history of Indian bronzes begins with the Indus-Sarasvatī civilization. The famous Dancing Girl of Mohenjodaro has become immortal despite the controversy regarding its true affiliation. The Daimabad (district Ahmednagar, Maharashtra) hoard betrays the continuity of the tradition even in the down southern part of the civilization and comprises some very important early bronzes. The state of Haryana possesses about half a century of typical and upward of 300 late Harappan sites but bronzes of the class of Mohenjodaro and Daimabad are yet to be discovered. That metal working started early in the region, is amply evidenced by the discovery of numerous implements of the 'Copper Hoard culture' from south-western Haryana, particularly from Hansi in district Hisar, now housed in the Gurukula Museums at Jhajjar and Narela, published by Paul Yule. Like all other parts of India, Haryana too seems to have lost the tradition around the middle of the second millennium BC.

The *Mahābhārata* speaks of an iron image (*āyasī-pratimā*) of Bhīma embraced and crushed by Dhṛitarāshṭra. The *Rāmāyaṇa* refers to the golden image of Sītā substituted for her during the performance of the Aśvamedha sacrifice by Rāma while she was in exile in Vālmīki's hermitage. The Dharma Sūtras also refer to the metal images. A person who committed sexual intercourse with his teacher's wife was required to embrace a metal image of a woman as penance. The Buddhist Jātakas contain numerous references to statues made of gold (*suvanna patimā*). Despite these literary references, however, there is a great paucity of the actual discoveries of the early metal images. The art of making metal images seems to have been revived in Bihar and the Deccan during the Kushāṇa-Sātavāhana period. The Jaina bronzes from Chausa

(Bihar) and lion, elephant riders, etc. from Brahmapuri (district Kolhapur, Maharashtra) are the interesting examples thereof.

References to metal images are more frequent from Gupta times. The *Nāyādhammakahāo,* a Jaina text of the Gupta period, refers to a life-size golden image of the princess Malli, who later became a tīrthaṅkara. The Jaina *Bṛihat-Kalpa-Bhāshya* (*circa* sixth century AD) speaks of a mechanical image of a human being, which could walk and open and shut its eyes. The *Matsya, Bhāgavata* and *Devī Purāṇa* refer to metal images. The actual finds also betray the popularity of this art. After the Kushāṇa period a refinement and more pleasing appearance is witnessed and the Gupta period denotes the highest attainment of purity in bodily form as well as serenity in facial features. Some Gandhāra impact too is discernible here and there. The Gupta influence did not remain confined to the empire but permeated into other parts of the country and even transcended the boundaries of the country. Gupta impact lingered on in the subsequent centuries also in some regions. It was, however, at the end of the post-Gupta phase (which ushered in the early medieval period) that we find an ever increasing production of bronzes in various parts of India.

Despite the fact that centres of metal images developed in the adjoining states of Rajasthan, Uttar Pradesh (including the recently carved out Uttaranchal), Himachal Pradesh and Jammu & Kashmir, the present day states of Haryana and Punjab (out of which Haryana was carved out in November 1966) remained terra incognita as far as bronze images are concerned. The fascinating discovery of the Hansi hoard has filled a great void and thrown very important and fresh light on the art of metal images, as well as on the religious conditions of the region in the early medieval period. The hoard has remained almost unknown to the outside world in spite of its having been discovered nearly two decades ago and is now preserved in the Digambara Jaina Temple at Hansi where it is difficult to study it properly and assess its significance. The present publication, it is hoped, will fulfil this desideratum.

Indian Institute of Advanced Study
Shimla – 171 005

Devendra Handa

Contents

Acknowledgements

I express my deep gratitude to Sarvashri O.P. Bharadwaj and L.K. Jain, both IAS, the then Director and Commissioner of the Department of Archaeology and Museums, Haryana, for taking me on deputation from the Panjab University, Chandigarh during 1984-85 as its Deputy Director. It was during this short stint that I not only made some important archaeological discoveries and acquisitions for the department myself but also made a first-hand study of all its hoarding and archaeological remains of Haryana and made many trips to Hansi. The subsequent Directors and Commissioners, Shri R.N. Prashar and Smt. Kiran Agrawal to mention particularly, were also kind enough to permit me to study and photograph the material whenever I made a request. I record my deep gratitude to all of them. When it was decided to hand over this wonderful hoard to the Jaina Sabhā of Hansi in January 1990, Shri A.D. Malik, IAS, the then Director of the department, invited me to photograph, study and publish the hoard. I am thus especially beholden to him. I am thankful to all old colleagues in the department, Sarvashri Madhava Acharya, J.S. Khatri, D.S. Malik, Dr. Surinder Arora and Bhup Singh to mention a few, who rendered all possible help whenever required. The photographs, both colour and black and white, were taken by my friend Mr. Surinder Dhami.

I am grateful to Prof. Ajay Mitra Shastri who has always been a source of inspiration and keenly interested in all my projects. Prof. C.S. Gupta of the Department of Ancient Indian History, Culture and Archaeology of the Nagpur University kindly lent me his copy of the *Akota Bronzes* which was so very essential to study this hoard of Jaina images. I have discussed some problems with Prof. R.C. Sharma, former Director-General of the National Museum, New Delhi and presently

Hon. Director, Jñāna-Pravāha, Varanasi and benefited from some of his suggestions. Prof. Ashvini Agrawal of the Panjab University, Chandigarh has been helpful in various ways. My sincere thanks to all of them.

Shri C. Dorje, Superintending Archaeologist of the Chandigarh Circle of the Archaeological Survey of India, has been helpful in various ways. His colleague, Mr. Vinod Kumar, prepared the map of Haryana, which has been utilized with slight modification here. I thank both of them. The map of important bronze sites of India has been copied from the 1988 Festival of India publication *The Great Tradition: Indian Bronze Masterpieces.* I thank the concerned authorities.

I am deeply indebted to Prof. V.C. Srivastava, Director, Indian Institute of Advanced Study, Shimla whose perceptions of Indology have been a source of inspiration to me and who has very kindly accepted this monograph to be included in the publications of the Institute. He has been very gracious to write the Foreword also.

I am beholden to Mr. Ashok Sharma, the all-purpose and resourceful PRO of the Institute, for making all arrangements regarding the publication of this monograph and liaising the work with the publisher. I owe special thanks to Mr. Vikas Arya and his entire team of the Aryan Books International, for the layout of the photographs and text and all their co-operation in the production of the monograph.

I owe more than what the words can express to my wife Avinash who took over all the onerous domestic duties and freed me to devote myself to my work and has been helpful in various ways in all my endeavours. It will be mere formality to thank my son Tushar for providing technical help at the computer whenever I required it, my daughter Vibha for helping me in the final selection of the photographs, and little Jahnavi, my *dauhitrī* and friend, who has delayed it like all my other projects but has provided the solace of life which is so very essential to live.

List of Illustrations

I

Introductory

HANSI — HISTORICAL BACKDROP

Hansi (long. 76° 19' E. and lat. 29° 6' N.) is situated on the Rewari-Bathinda section of the Northern Railway, 122 km north-west of the former and 186 km south-east of the latter. Now the tahsil headquarters of district Hisar, it is connected by road with Delhi (via Rohtak), Jind, Tohana, Hisar, Tosham and Bhiwani (Map 1). Western Yamuna Canal which runs quite close to the town of Hansi was dug out by Firoz Tughlaq in the old bed of the Ṛigvedic river Dṛishadvatī. Antiquity of Hansi is evidenced by a huge mound, measuring more than a thousand feet square, to the north of the present town, with the ruined and dilapidated walls of a strong and massive fort still extant at places, as wide as 37 feet and as high as 52 feet. The fort was almost entirely dismantled after 1857 and its material was sold out. An old gateway, called Barsi Darwaza, however, has survived with its guard-room. There is enough of evidence to believe that the town was fortified in the ancient times and the fortification wall was repaired, renovated and reinforced from time to time.

At various stages in its history Hansi has been known variously as Asi, Āsī, Āsidurga, Āsīgarh, Āsikā, Āśikā, Āṃsī, Hansi, etc. and there are different anecdotes and local traditions to derive these names from Assa Jat, king Assajit (Aśvajit) of the lunar dynasty, the laughter (*haṃsī*) of Ambā, the daughter of kind Anaṅgpāla, etc.[1] The tradition that the city derives its name from the Sanskrit word *asi* (sword), the famous product of the place, which was in great demand for its quality, is worthy of note. Even the sword of Muhammad Sahib, Zulfikār, is said to have gone from here.[2] The tradition of metal working at Hansi goes back to the proto-historic period as it has yielded a large number

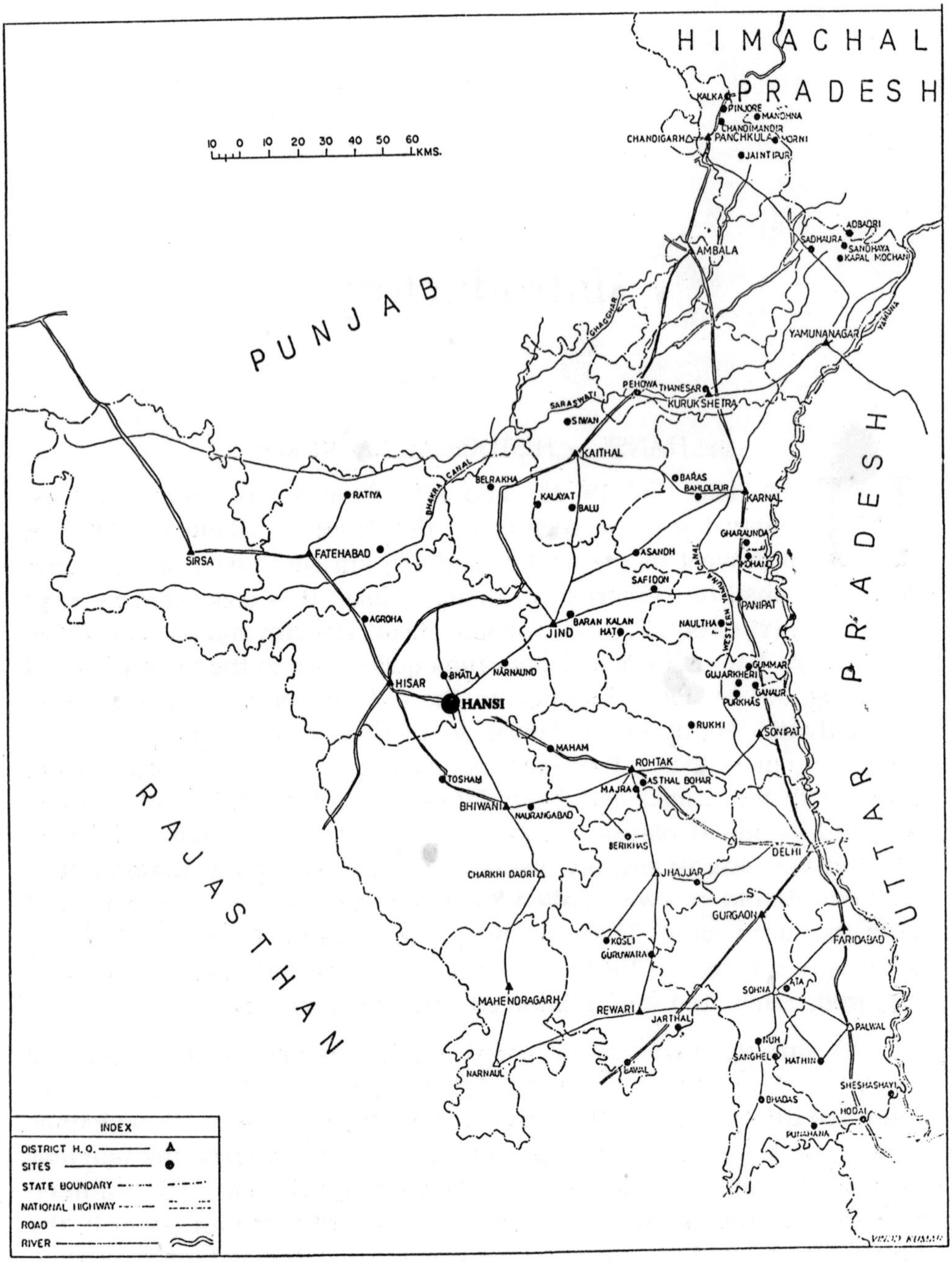

Map 1. Haryana: Location of Hansi and other sites yielding art relics

of copper/bronzes axes, celts, swords, bars, harpoons, etc.[3] Painted Grey Ware, generally associated with the Aryans and dated to about the first half of the first millennium BC, has also been found from Hansi.[4] Prinsep regarded the Aśokan pillar now standing in the Gujri Mahal of Hisar fort to have originally belonged to Hansi.[5] Cunningham also held this view.[6] If this observation is correct, Hansi must have been a flourishing town in Aśoka's time.[7] It was probably a stronghold of the Kushāṇas also.[8] Yaudheya coins have been recovered from Hansi in considerable numbers.[9] The continuity of the settlement is indicated by the discovery of Kota, Ādivarāha, Tomara and Chauhan coins as well as numerous stone sculptures and other remains.[10] An inscription dated V.S. 1224 and belonging to the Chauhan king Pṛithvīrāja II (now in the Royal Scottish Museum) has also been found from Hansi.[11] The town has got several Muslim inscriptions and monuments too.[12]

The *Tarikh-i-Subuktigin* of Abul Fazl al-Baikhaki makes a special reference to its invincible fort and the stiff resistance it offered during a siege of ten days to Masud before its capture on the first day of AD 1038.[13] The *Tabaqat-i-Nasiri* of Minhajuddin mentions Hansi as the capital of the province of Siwalik[14] but with the foundation of Hisar-i-Firoza, it was reduced to the position of an *iqta* only.[15] It became a great religious centre of the Sufis during the Tughlaq period.[16] During the subsequent Sultanate and Mughal period, it continued to exist experiencing vicissitudes but the famine of 1783 left Hansi in partial ruins till George Thomas seized it in 1795 and revived it.[17] It became a cantonment for some time after the British occupation[18] and has lived on to the present day.

DISCOVERY OF THE HOARD

Though the surrounding states of Rajasthan, Uttar Pradesh, Himachal Pradesh, Jammu & Kashmir had all yielded important bronzes yet the present states of Haryana and Punjab had been the terra incognita as far as bronze images are concerned (Map 2). It was in February 1982 that a big hoard of bronzes was found accidentally by some boys whose ball, with which they were playing, fell in a rain gully and one of them descended into it in search of the ball. He saw some metallic object looking out from the exposed section of the mound and pulled it. To his surprise, it was an image. Some of his fellow mates also followed him and took away whatsoever came into their hands. The news of this find spread like a wildfire and before the police reached the spot, the whole of the treasure had vanished. However, the police did not

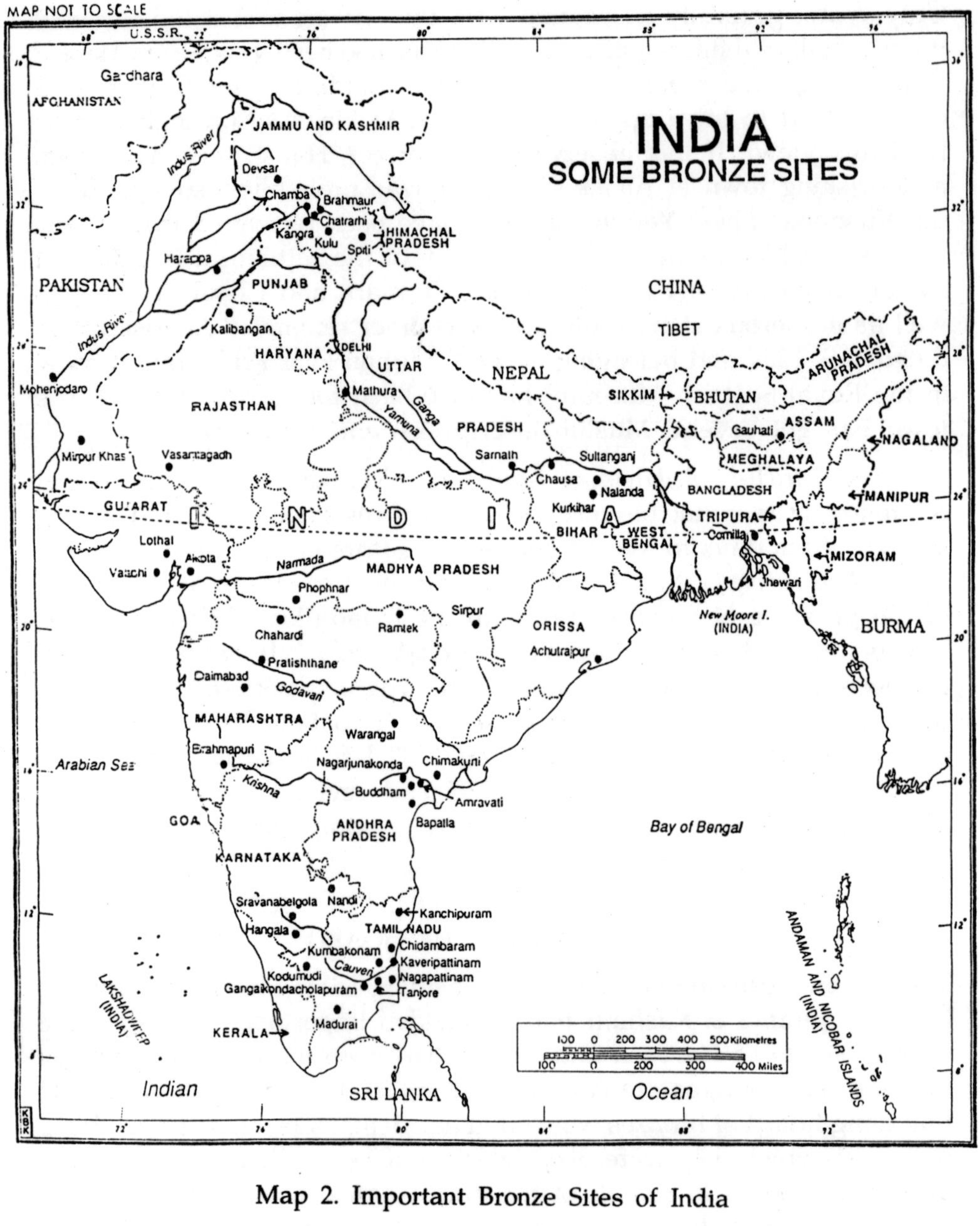

Map 2. Important Bronze Sites of India

lose much time to swing into action and could recover fifty-eight pieces including some *loṭās* (water vessels), a sacrificial ladle (*arghyā*), a conch, and a *pīṭhikā* 'pedestal' besides the big copper cauldron (*deg*) in which they lay actually buried. The Department of Archaeology and Museums, Haryana acquired this hoard under Treasure Trove Act. Local citizens, however, believe that the actual number of bronzes in the *deg* and looted by the people must have been more than one hundred, hundred eight as one gentleman informed me during one of my visits to Hansi.[19] I was invited in January 1990 to photograph, study and publish the hoard by Shri A.D. Malik (IAS), the then Director of the Department when it was to be handed over to the Jaina community of Hansi. At the intervention of the Archaeological Survey of India, this transfer of the hoard was postponed but the bronzes were ultimately made over to the representatives of Shri Digambar Jain Sabha, Hansi for being displayed in a museum at Hansi on 30th December, 1991. The break-up of the bronzes is as follows[20]—

Ādinātha (Ṛishabhanātha)	4
Mallinātha	2
Chandraprabha	2
Pārśvanātha	20
Mahāvīra	6
Unidentified Jinas	5
Sarvatobhadrikās	3
Parents of Jinas	1
Jaina Āchārya (?)	1
Achchhuptā	2
Sarasvatī	4
Bhūmisparśa Buddha	1
Avalokiteśvara	1
Pīṭhikā (pedestal)	1
Attendant figures	2
Loṭās (water vessels)	2 (plus some broken pieces)
Arghyā (ladle)	1

We thus see that basically it is a Jaina hoard of bronzes though at the time of distress the Buddhists too joined the Jainas in burying their sacred icons to save them from sacrilege.

JAINISM IN HARYANA

Jainism is a religion of hoary antiquity. The Jainas believe it to be eternal, having been revealed repeatedly by twenty-four Tīrthaṅkaras, of which the last two are certainly historical figures. Pārśva, the penultimate pontiff, lived between 877 and 777 BC and the last tīrthaṅkara Mahāvīra died 250 years after him, i.e., in 527 BC.[21]

Jaina tradition holds that the first tīrthaṅkara Ṛishabhanātha turned the wheel of the Jaina faith at Takshaśilā,[22] but archaeological excavations have revealed that Taxila did not come into existence before the sixth-fifth century BC.[23] The tradition is, thus, not compatible with historical and archaeological evidence. Similarly, the legend of Ṛishabhanātha's visit to the Yavana country, i.e., Iyonia, a Greek country of West Asia, is also contradicted by facts of archaeology and history as the Iyonian kingdom was not established before the eighth century BC.[24] Obviously, the tradition of the tīrthaṅkaras having visited north-west India is as apocryphal as that of Buddha having visited it.[25]

Some scholars try to find reference to Jainism in the Vedic literature and some others suggest the existence of Jainism in the Harappan times on the basis of the torso of a nude male, certain motifs and postures. There is, however, nothing to commend such a hypothesis, as not even a shred of evidence has been available regarding the prevalence of Jainism during the whole of the second millennium BC and even subsequently till the rise of Pārśvanātha. It has rightly been observed that "when we go beyond Pārśva, we get into a realm of legend, both in regard to unbelievable differences of time that elapsed between each of the preceding tīrthaṅkaras and the description of their personage", and that it would not "be cogent to accord an absolute and acceptable time-scale to the tīrthaṅkaras prior to Pārśva or accept their historicity in the present state of our knowledge."[26]

The westernmost cities visited by Pārśva include Kauśāmbī, Ahichchhatrā and Hastināpura which all have been excavated and were in existence during his time. Though the Jaina tradition associates Supārśvanātha (7th tīrthaṅkara), Neminātha (21st tīrthaṅkara), Arishṭanemi (22nd tīrthaṅkara) and Mahāvīra (24th tīrthaṅkara) with Mathurā, yet there is no evidence to prove that Jainism got any firm footing at Mathurā before the second century BC. The *Uttarādhyayana Sūtra* records that Mahāvīra had advised the Jaina monks not to roam beyond Thūṇā which was situated on the western boundary of Āryadeśa, later called Madhyadeśa, perhaps because Jainism had not penetrated beyond this site by that time.[27] Thūṇā is generally identified with Thanesar (ancient Sthāṇvīśvara). No Tīrthaṅkara seems to have ever visited Haryana.[28]

The Nandas had patronized Jainism to some extent. Chandragupta Maurya had strong leanings towards Jainism. Megasthenes, the Greek Ambassador to his court, mentions Sarmanes, i.e., Śramaṇas, probably the Jaina monks.[29] Bindusāra does not seem to have been inclined towards Jainism as the Jaina sources are silent about him.[30] Aśoka was more favourable to Buddhism but his spirit of toleration and broadmindedness is reflected in his instructions that the Brāhmaṇas, Śramaṇas, Nirgranthas and Ājīvikas should be given due honour and care.[31] Since the Nirgranthas have been mentioned only in his Seventh Pillar Edict engraved on the Delhi-Topra pillar which was brought to Firoz Shah Kotla, Delhi by Sultan Firoz Tughlaq from the village Topra near Jagadhari in district Yamunanagar of Haryana, A.K. Roy thinks that by the time of Aśoka, the Jaina religion had spread as far as Haryana.[32]

The Jaina texts are, however, eloquent about Kuṇāla, his son. About 20 km north-east of Fatehabad exists a village of the name of Kunal which has recently been excavated and has yielded pre-, transitional and mature Harappan relics of great importance.[33] The upper strata has unfortunately completely been removed by recent agricultural activities but the discovery of Painted Grey Ware and later sherds from the fields indicate that it continued to flourish even subsequently. Though archaeological excavations at the site have not yielded any Jaina relics yet there is a local tradition that the Mauryan pillar now standing in the courtyard of the ldgah at Fatehabad was brought here from Kunal. It may be mentioned here that Rodgers had come across Jaina relics at Fatehabad during his survey of the site in 1888.[34]

Kuṇāla's son Samprati contributed greatly to the spread of Jainism.[35] Roy refers to the founding of the Uddeha-gaṇa by Rohaṇa, a disciple of the Jaina monk Suhastin who was a contemporary of Samprati. Uddeha-gaṇa was divided into four *śākhās* 'branches' one of which was Udambarika. Roy connects it with the Audumbaras, whose capital was Pratishṭhāna, i.e., Pathankot.[36] Audumbara coinage,[37] however, does not show any impact of Jainism nor is there any other evidence to prove the identity of the Udumbarika branch of the Jaina Uddeha-gaṇa with the Audumbaras. Roy seems to have been misled by the sound analogy as the Audumbaras are known to have descended from Viśvamitra, a connection revealed by their coins,[38] and also because their coins show a Śaiva temple depicted on them. The Audumbara rulers bore Śaiva names too.

Jainism, however, seems to have been in a flourishing state at Mathurā during the second century BC.[39] Whether it was popular in the contiguous region of southern Haryana also or not remains yet to be proved by future discoveries.[40] A Jaina patriarch Lohāchārya is said to have propagated Jainism amongst the mercantile tribe of Agroha (i.e., Agrodaka *Janapada*) during the first century AD.[41] *Therīgāthā*, which forms part of the *Khuddakanikāya*, contains stanzas of Nanduttarā and Mittakali (five each) of Kururaṭṭha. The traditional mention of names with the lives of the *Bhikshuṇīs* 'nuns' is preserved in the commentary of Dhammapāla known as the *Parmatthadīpinī*, ascribable to the fifth century AD. Both the *therīs* (nuns) belonged to the Brāhmaṇa families of Kammāsadamma *nigama* 'corporation' in the Kuru country. Nanduttarā had earlier been initiated to Jainism.[42] There is, however, complete paucity of archaeological evidence regarding the prevalence of Jainism in Haryana during the Kushāṇa and even Gupta period as no Jaina inscription, icon or *āyāga-paṭa* has so far been discovered from the region. John Marshall had exposed some *stūpas* in Sirkap, the second city of Taxila, which he associated with Jainism.[43] The association, however, is very doubtful.[44]

Jaina relics of Gupta art tradition found from Murti in district Jhelum of Pakistan[45] and the presence of the Jainas in the Gandhāra region as recorded by Hiuen Tsiang,[46] however, reveal that Jainism must have spread to those areas after having traversed the present day Haryana and Punjab states of India. The earliest archaeological evidence of the spread of Jainism in Haryana, however, comes from Hansi.

CONTENTS AND TECHNIQUE

From the list of contents of the hoard given above, we have seen that Pārśvanātha has been the most popular tīrthaṅkara worshipped at Hansi. We, however, feel that most of the unidentified Jina figures may actually be those of Mahāvīra. If it is so, Mahāvīra may have been the next most popular Jina followed by Ādinātha, Chandraprabha and

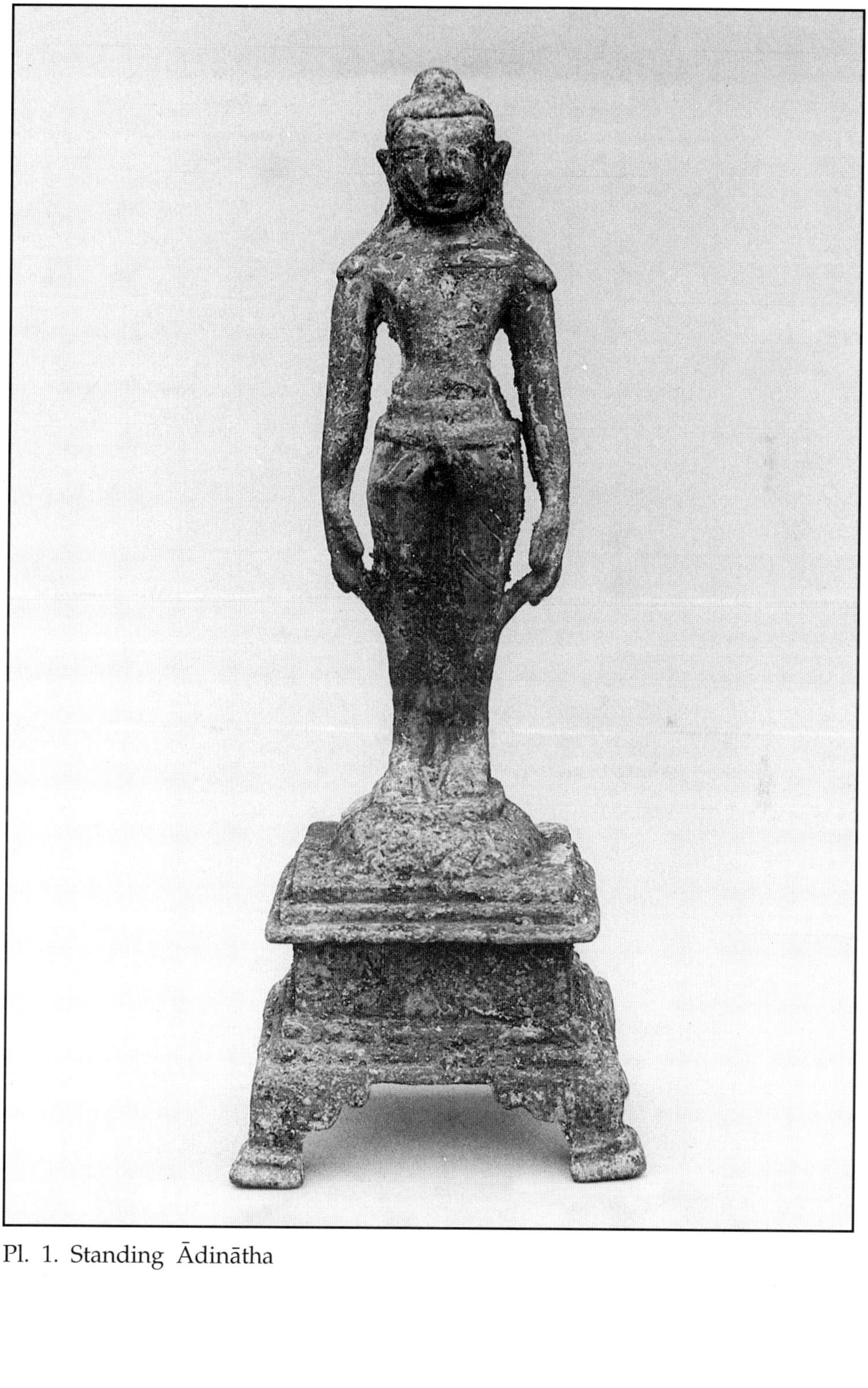

Pl. 1. Standing Ādinātha

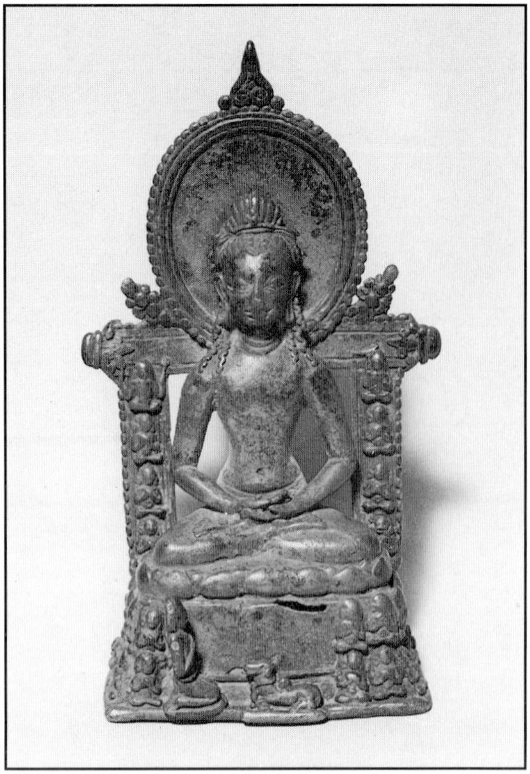

Pl. 2a. *Padmāsana* Ādinātha

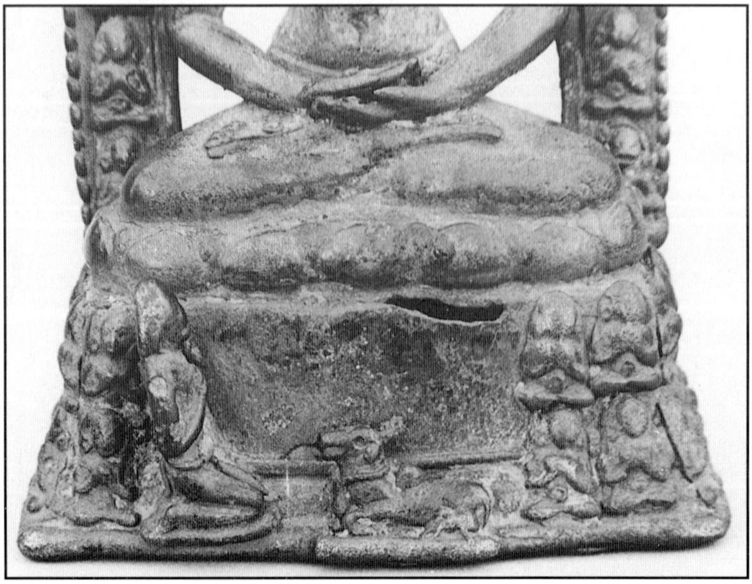

Pl. 2b

Pls. 2b-e. Details of the pedestal, side and back views

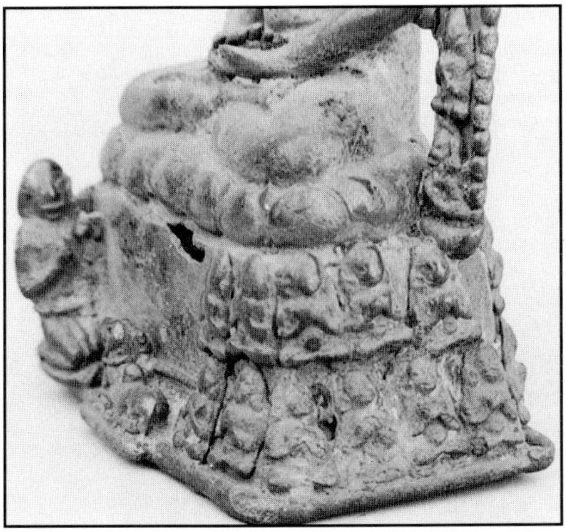

Pl. 2c

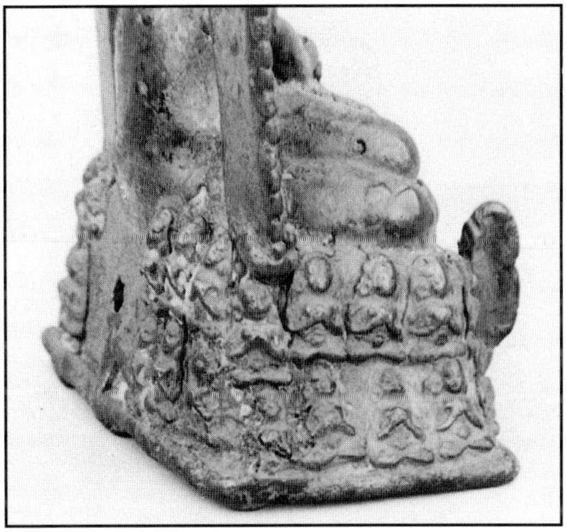

Pl. 2d

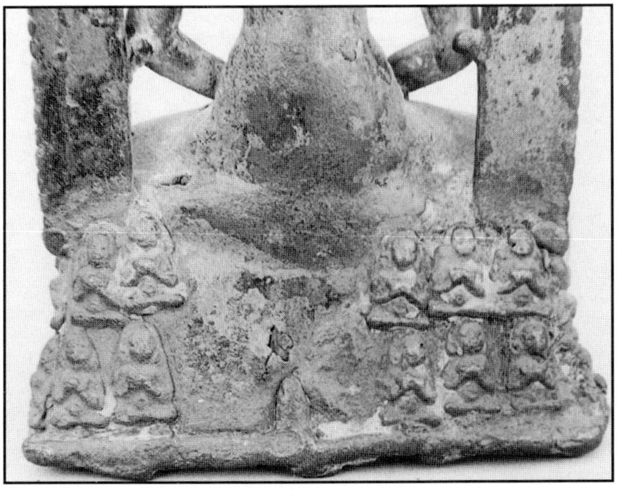

Pl. 2e

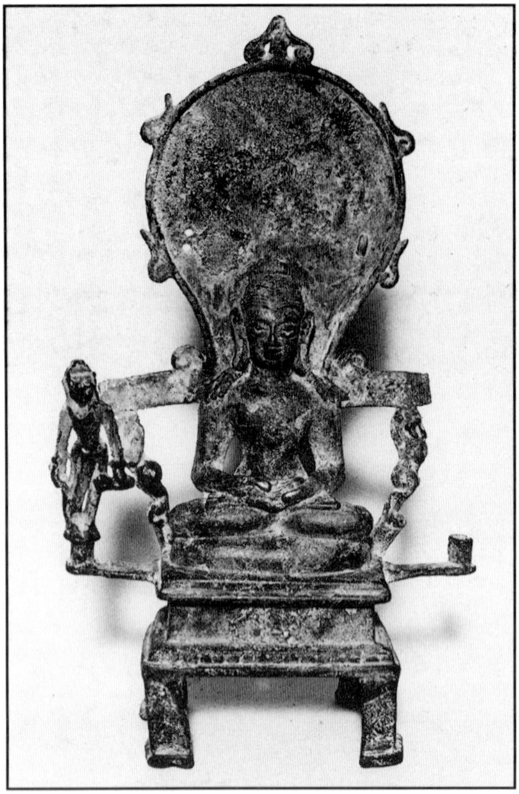

Pl. 3. *Padmāsana* Ādinātha

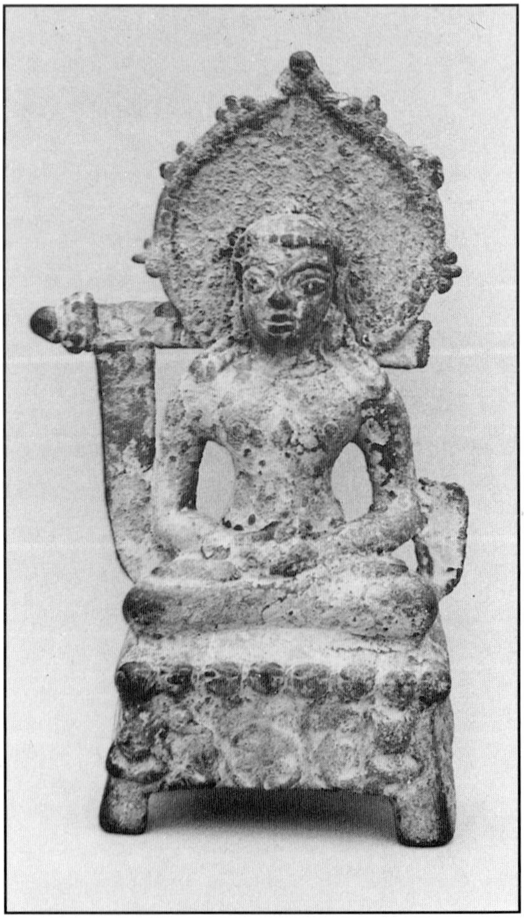

Pl. 4. *Padmāsana* Ādinātha on a *siṃhāsana*

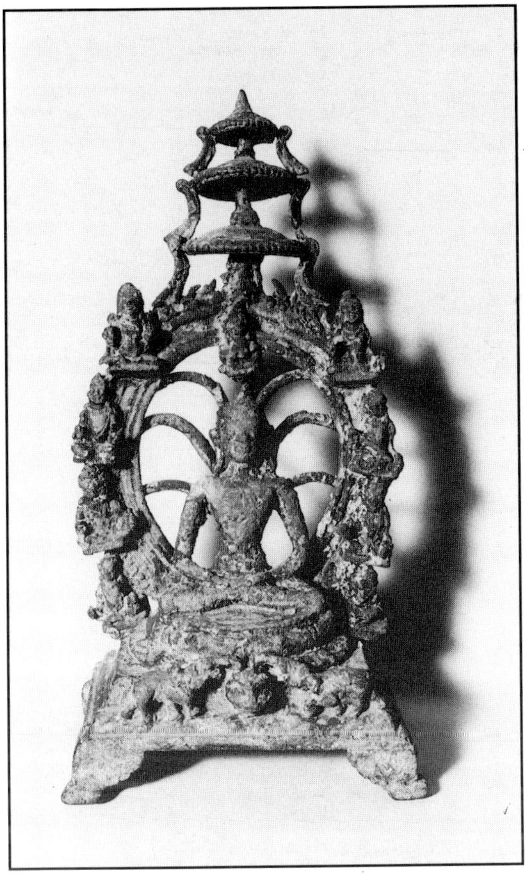

Pl. 5. Mallinātha

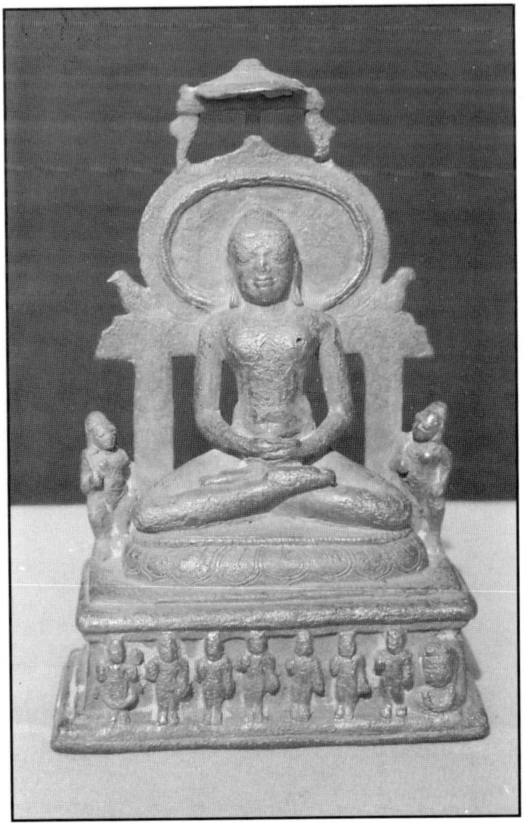

Pl. 6. Female Mallinātha

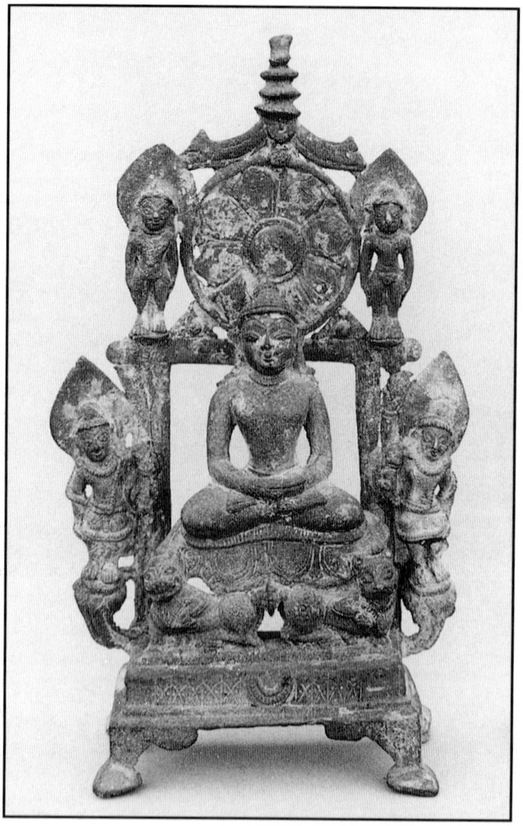

Pl. 7a. *Padmāsana* Chandraprabha

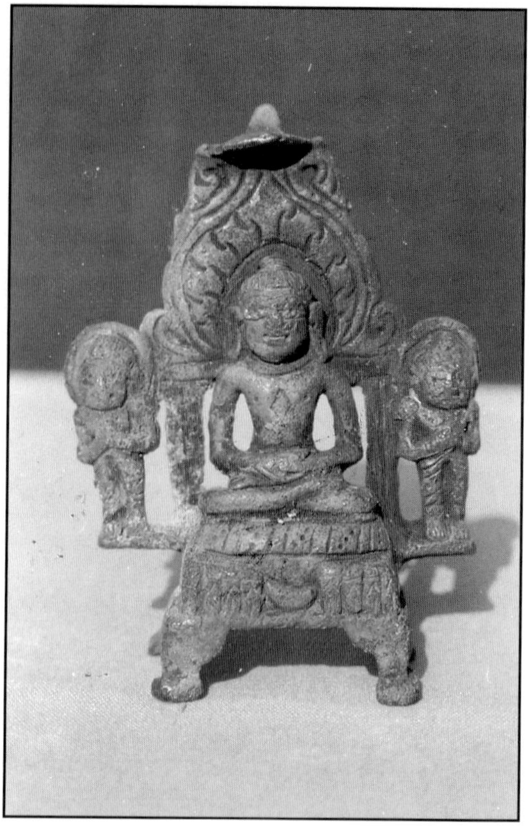

Pl. 8. *Padmāsana* Chandraprabha

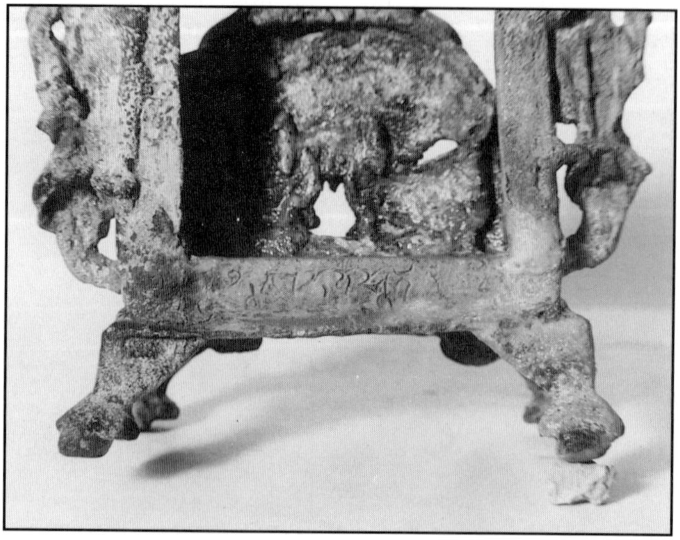

Pl. 7b. Inscription at the back

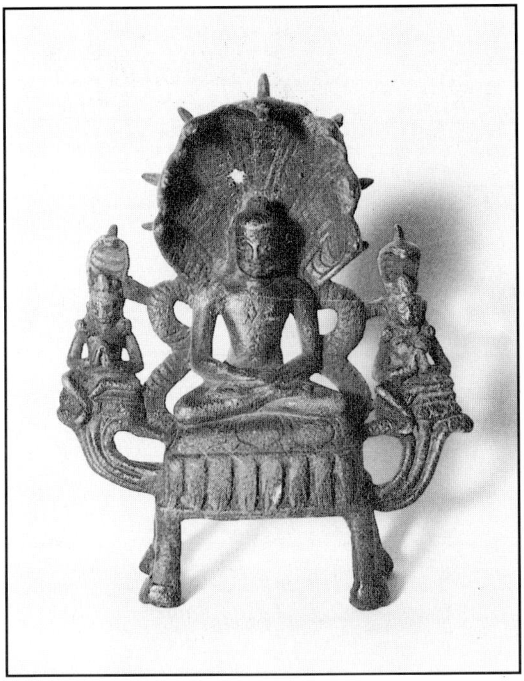

Pl. 9

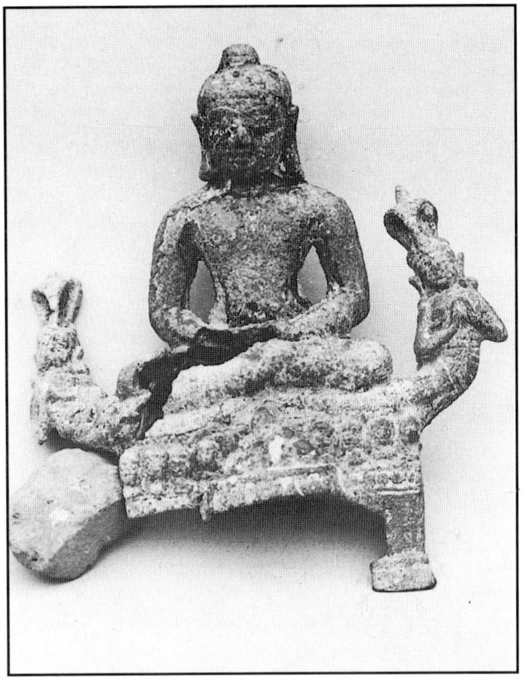

Pl. 10

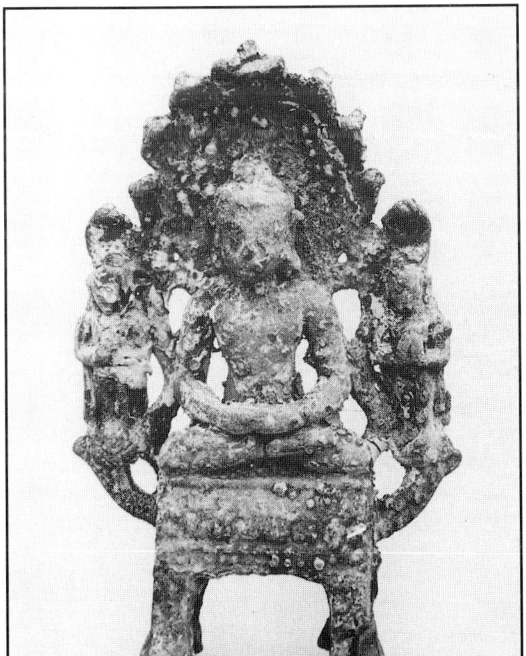

Pl. 11

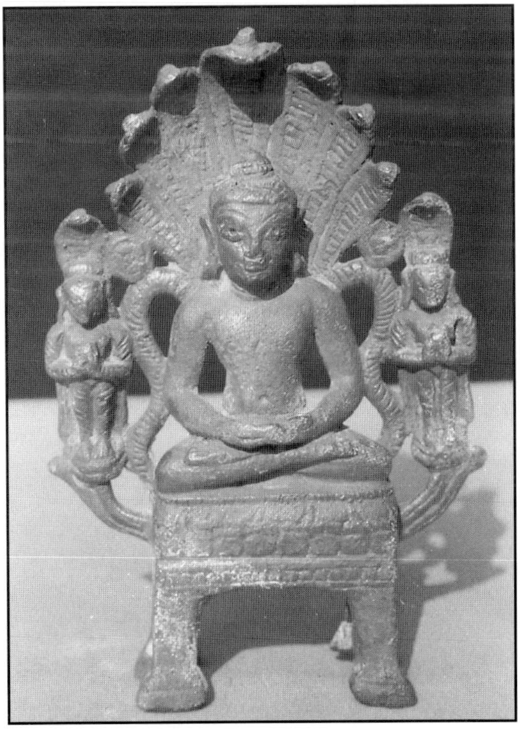

Pl. 12

Pls. 9-12. *Padmāsana* Pārśvanātha with serpent-hooded attendants

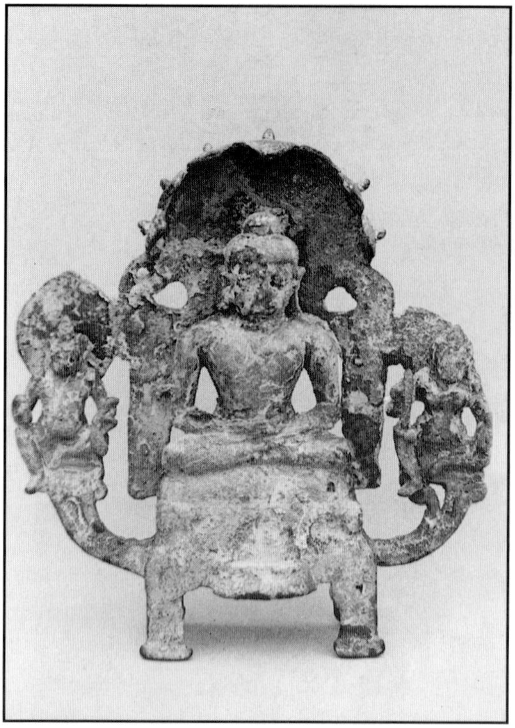

Pl. 13

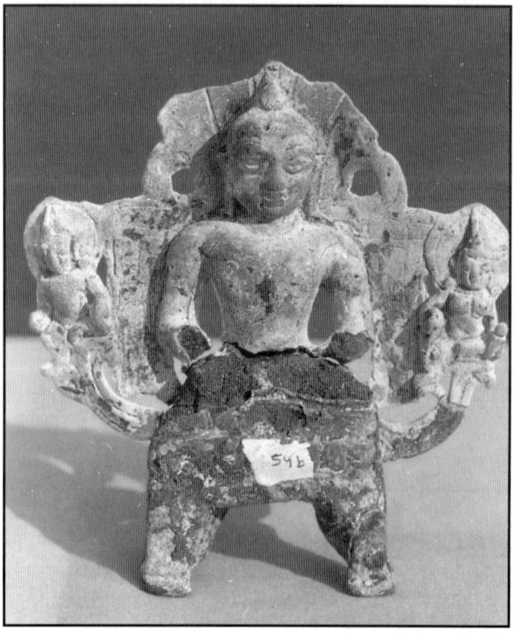

Pl. 14

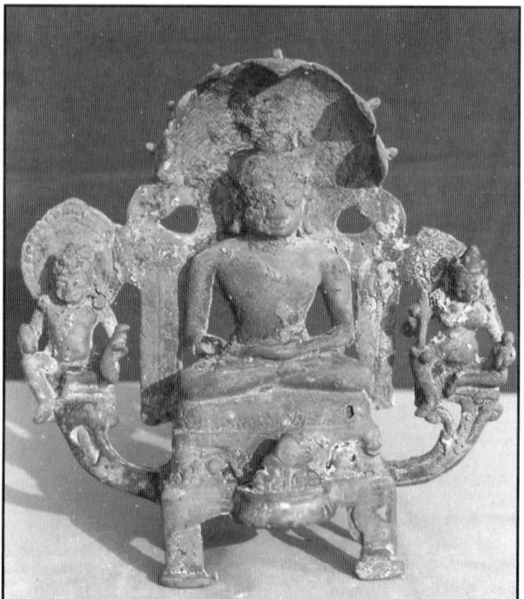

Pl. 15

Pls. 13-15. *Padmāsana* Pārśvanātha with Sarvānubhūti and Ambikā

Mallinātha. Surprisingly no independent image of Neminātha has been recovered in the hoard though he may have been one of the tīrthaṅkaras depicted in the *Sarvatobhadrikās*; but since no emblems exist on the pedestals it is difficult to make any statement with certitude. The two water vessels, one of them being channel spouted, the *arghyā* and the conch[47] may have actually been used in the rituals of worship.

The images of *bhūmisparśa* 'earth-touching' Buddha and Avalokiteśvara Padmapāṇi[48] reveal that the hoard is not exclusively Jaina and that though a prominent Jaina centre, other religious faiths too flourished side by side at Hansi.

Actually all the images are not made of bronze and to call them as bronzes is a misnomer. The *kāyotsarga* Ādinātha (Pl. 1) contains more of iron and other impurities and has consequently turned bluish brown. A *tri-tīrthikā* of Pārśvanātha (Pl. 19) has also grown bluish on treatment because of considerable iron content. Image of Ādinātha (Pl. 3), Chandraprabha (Pl. 7), *tri-tīrthikās* of Pārśvanātha (Pls. 15-18), *Sarvatobhadrikā* (Pl. 38), etc. seem to be made of copper while a Jina (Pl. 36) is a real bronze. Most of the images at the time of our examination had a thick encrustation of corrosion indicating different metal contents of these images. They have, however, been treated subsequently. Since the term 'bronze' is popularly used for metal images in general, it has been used here also knowing fully well that it is a misnomer.

Also different methods of preparing them have been used. Ādinātha (Pl. 1) is fully solid cast but most of the images have been hollow cast (Pls. 2, 6, 10, 11, etc.). The pedestals, back-slabs, halos, triple umbrellas, subsidiary or attendant figures, serpent-hoods over Pārśvanātha, upper parts of the *sarvatobhadrikās,* etc. were cast separately. There are instances in which the back-slabs were provided by beaten and cut sheets with incised patterns or decorations (*samghāima*) as also referred to in the *Aṇuyogadvāra Sūtra*[49] and the *Nāyādhammakahāo*[50] (a Jaina text of the Gupta period). Hinges at the back of some of these images were provided for the rods of the triple umbrella. The cognizance bull on the pedestal of the image of Ādinātha (Pl. 2) is riveted whereas a hole on another (Pl. 3) indicates that it was meant for riveting the cognizance. The undergarment can be made out only in the image of Ādinātha (Pl. 1) and some subsidiary images of the Jinas in the *tri-tīrthikās* (Pl. 19-25, etc.). We thus see that both the Digambara and the Śvetāmbara sects flourished side by side at Hansi and at the time of the calamity of burying the images, the Digambaras, Śvetāmbaras and even the Buddhists joined together.

NOTES AND REFERENCES

1. For details, see Aditya Lohan, *A Historico-Cultural Study of the Hansi Region (from the Earliest Times to A.D. 1526)*, Ph. D. Thesis (Unpublished), Kurukshetra University, Kurukshetra, 1988.
2. Bhup Singh Rajput, *Souvenir on Hansi*, August, 1981, p. 6.
3. These copper hoard implements have been collected by Swami Omanand Sarasvati and housed in the Jhajjar and Narela (Kanya) Gurukula. Paul Yule has made an in- depth study of these implements in his book *Metal Work of the Bronze Age in India*, Munchen, 1985. Aditya Lohan (*op. cit.*, pp 254-60, Pls. XI-XIII) and R.C. Agrawala ('Celts from Hansi, Haryana,' *Kusumañjali — New Interpretation of Indian Art & Culture: Sh. C. Sivaramamurti Commemoration Volume*, edited by M.S. Nagaraja Rao, Vol. I, Delhi, 1987, pp. 15-16, Pls. 1-6) have also tried to highlight the importance of these finds.
4. *Indian Archaeology 1963-64 — A Review*, p. 90.
5. *Journal of the Royal Asiatic Society of Bengal*, Vol. VII, p. 430.
6. Alexander Cunningham, *Archaeological Survey of India, Report for the Year 1872-73*, Vol. V (Reprint, Varanasi, 1966), p. 142.
7. B. Ch. Chhabra, "Aśokan Pillar at Hissar, Panjab", *Vishveshvaranand Indological Journal*, Vol. II, Pt. ii (Sept. 1964), pp. 319-22.
8. There is the possibility of this pillar having been shifted to its present place from Agroha, the city destroyed by Firoz Tughlaq, whose materials he utilized in the construction of the fort and the city founded by him in AD 1354. See also Devendra Handa, *Heritage of Haryana: Buddhist Remains*, Chandigarh, 1989, p. 12.
9. *Imperial Gazetteer of India*, Vol. I, p. 229.
10. Alexander Cunningham, *Ancient Geography of India* (Reprint, Varanasi, 1963), p. 207; John Allan, *Catalogue of the Coins of Ancient India*, London, 1936 (Indian Reprint, Delhi, 1975), p. cli; Acharya Bhagwan Deva, *Vīra-bhūmi Hariyānā* (Hindi), Jhajjar, 1965, pp. 127, 134-35; *Jana Sāhitya*, Patiala, Vol. IV, Nos. 10-11, pp. 347-48; *Annual Report of the Archaeological Survey of India 1922-23*, p. 92, Pl. V; Devendra Handa, "Mahisha-suramardini in the Medieval Art of Haryana", in *Researches in Indian Archaeology, Art, Architecture, Culture and Religion (Vijaya Kanta Mishra Commemoration Volume)*, ed. By P. K. Mishra, Delhi, 1995, Vol. II, pp. 279-89, Pls. 73-96; 'Varāha Images from Haryana,' in *Researches in Indian History, Archaeology, Art and Religion (Prof. Upendra Thakur Felicitation Volume)*, edited by G. Kuppuram and K. Kumudmani, Vol. I, Delhi, 1990,

p. 87, Pl. 50.

11. D.R. Bhandarkar, List of Brāhmī Inscriptions of Northern India (Appendix to *Epigraphia Indica*, Vols. XIX-XXIII), Calcutta, 1912, p. 49, No. 329.

12. H.B.W. Garrick, *Archaeological Survey Report*, Vol. XXIII, pp. 13-19.

13. H.M. Elliot and J. Dowson, *History of India as told by its own Historians*, Vol. II, p. 125ff.

14. *Tabaqat-i-Nasiri*, Eng. Tr. by H.C. Raverty (Reprint, Delhi, 1981). See also M.S. Ahluwalia, "Medieval Hansi", *Proceedings of the Punjab History Congress,* Sixth Session, Patiala (March 19-20, 1971), pp. 95-103.

15. Shams Siraj Afif, *Tarikh-i-Firuzshahi*, Calcutta, 1890, pp. 124ff.

16. S.A.A. Rizvi, *Tughlaq Kālīna Bhārata* (Hindi), Part I, Aligarh, 1956, pp. 145 ff.

17. W. Franklin, *The Military Memoirs of George Thomas*, London, 1803. See also C. Grey, *European Adventurers of Northern India (1785-1849)*, edited by H.L.O. Garret, Lahore, 1929, pp. 43ff; Shelford Bidwel, *Swords for Hire*, London, 1971, p. 131.

18. *Gazetteer of Hissar District*, Lahore, 1883-84, pp. 8ff.

19. This information has been gathered from the officials of the Department of Archaeology and Museums, Haryana and some local citizens.

20. The list is at variance from our preliminary study of the bronzes (see Devendra Handa, "Jaina Bronze Hoard from Hansi — A Preliminary Study", in *The Bounteous Tree: Treasures in Indian Art and Culture*, edited by K. K. Chakravarty, Vol. II, Delhi, 1997, pp. 293-302, Pls. 1-14) and *Roopa-Lekha*, Vols. LXVII-LXXI (March 2001), pp. 1-13 and is based on our final scrutiny of all the available evidence.

21. M.N. Deshpande, "The Background and Tradition", in *Jaina Art And Architecture*, edited by A. Ghosh, Vol. I, New Delhi, 1974 (henceforth *JAA*), p. 16. Some scholars place Mahāvīra's *nirvāṇa* 'death' in 467 BC. For a discussion of the various theories regarding the dates of the death of Buddha and Mahāvīra and their contemporaneity, see Muni-Śrī Nagarāja, *Mahāvīra aura Buddha kī samasāmayikatā* (Hindi), Delhi, 1971.

22. Muni Kāntisāgara, *Khaṇḍaharo kā Vaibhava* (Hindi), 2nd ed., Banaras, 1959, p. 59.

23. John Marshall, *Taxila*, 3 Vols., Cambridge, 1951; *Guide to Taxila*, Cambridge, 1960.

24. *JAA*, I, p. 4, fn. 2.

25. *Ibid.* Also see Samuel Beal, *Buddhist Records of the Western World*, London, 1884, I, p. 235 and *Life of Hiuen-Tsiang by Hwui-Li*, London, 1882, p. 91.

26. Deshpande, *op. cit.*, p. 21.

27. *Sacred Books of the East*, Vol. XVII, pp. 38-39; V. Fausboll, *The Jataka*, London, 1963, Vol. VI, p. 62.

28. O.P. Bharadwaj, *Studies in the Historical Geography of Ancient India*, Delhi, 1986, p. 154.

29. J.W. McCrindle, *Ancient India as Described by Megasthenes and Arrian*, Revised 2nd ed., Calcutta, 1960, pp. 98 ff.

30. The *Divyāvadāna* (ed. by Cowell and Neil), ch. 27, pp. 544-86) refers to Bimbisāra sending a painting of Buddha to Rudrāyaṇa, king of Roruka. According to the Śvetāmbara tradition, Sthūlabhadra, a contemporary of Bindusāra, assumed the leadership of the *Saṅgha* after Bhadrabāhu's departure, and convened a council at Pāṭaliputra after the famine (which had occurred during the reign of Chandragupta Maurya) to put in order the sacred lore that had fallen in a state of decay (Jyoti Prasad Jain, *The Jaina Sources of the History of Ancient India*, Delhi, 1964, p. 105). There is, however, no evidence to show that Bindusāra favoured any particular religion.

31. E. Hultzsch, "Delhi-Topra Pillar Edicts", *Corpus Inscriptionum Indicarum*, Vol. I, London, 1925, pp. 119-37.

32. A.K. Roy, *A History of the Jainas*, New Delhi, 1984, p. 75.

33. J.S. Khatri and M. Acharya, "Kunal — A New Indus-Sarasvati Site", *Purātattva*, No. 25, pp. 84-86; S.P. Gupta, *The Indus-Sarasvati Civilization*, Delhi, 1996.

34. C.J. Rodgers, *Revised List of Objects of Archaeological Interest in the Panjab*, Lahore, 1891, p. 71.

35. *JAA*, I, p. 26.

36. Roy, *op. cit.*, pp. 75-76.

37. John Allan, *op. cit.*, pp. lxxxiii-lxxxvii and 122ff.

38. K.K. Dasgupta, *Tribal History of Ancient India — A Numismatic Approach*, Calcutta, 1974, pp. 43-44.

39. *JAA*, I, p. 51.

40. A systematic survey of southern Haryana is a great desideratum to ascertain its connection with Mathurā.

41. Jyoti Prasad Jain, *op. cit.*, p. 106.

42. *Therīgāthā*, which forms part of the *Khuddaka-nikāya*, contains stanzas of Nanduttarā and Mittakālī (five each), of Kururaṭṭha. The traditional mention of the names with the lives of the Bhikshuṇīs 'nuns' is preserved in the commentary of Dhammapāla known as the *Paramatthadīpanī*, ascribable to the fifth century AD. Both the *therīs*

'female recluses' belonged to the Kammāsadamma *nigama* 'corporation' in the Kuru country. Kammāsadamma is identified with village Kamaspur in Haryana by Bharadwaj (*op. cit.*, pp. 157-58). Nanduttarā had earlier been initiated to Jainism — *Imasmiṃ buddhuppāde Kururaṭṭhe Kammāsadamma-nigame brāhmaṇa-kule nibbattitvā ekachchānaṃ vijjāṭṭhānāni sippāyatanāni cha ugga-hetvā nigaṇṭhapabbajjaṃ upagaṃtvā vādasutā jambusākhaṃ gahetvā bhaddā...* (*Therīgāthā*, ed. N. K. Bhagwat, Bombay, 1956, p. 63).

43. Marshall (1960), *op. cit.*, pp. 69ff.

44. *JAA*, I, p. 8, fn. 2.

45. Murti was discovered by Aurel Stein and Fred. H. Andrews in 1889 and was revisited by Stein and Fabri in 1931. Yuan Chwang had also seen a Jaina temple there (Thomas Watters, *On Yuan Chwang's Travels in India*, Delhi, 1961, 1st Indian ed., pp. 250 ff). The remains of this and other fanes recovered by Stein were removed to the Central Museum, Lahore. For details see *Punjab District Gazetteer: Jhelum District*, Lahore, 1907, p. 45; M.A. Stein, *Archaeological Reconnaissances in North-Western India and South-Eastern Iran*, London, 1937, pp. 52-57, Pls. 20-21; Charles Fabri, "Archaeology in the Punjab", *Marg*, X (2), March 1957, p. 13; etc.

46. Watters, *op. cit.*

47. Cf. A conch engraved with the figure of Mahāvīra and his eleven *gaṇadharas* in the L.D. Institute, Ahmedabad. See for details U. P. Shah (Ed.), *Treasures of Jaina Bhaṇḍāras*, Ahmedabad, 1978, p. 97, No. 585, Pl. LXXIII.

48. Devendra Handa, "Two Buddhist Bronzes from Hansi", in *Buddhist Art and Thought*, edited by K.K. Mittal & Ashvini Agrawal, New Delhi, 1993, pp. 71-75, Pls. H 1 & 2.

49. *Aṇuyogadvāra Sūtra*, *sūtra* 10, Bombay, 1921, p. 1. See also *Aṇuyogadvāra Chūrṇī with Vṛitti*, Ratlam, 1928, pp. 7-8.

50. *Nāyādhammakahāo* (edited by N.V. Vaidya), Poona, 1940, p. 142.

II

The Images

A. JAINA IMAGES

Ādinātha

Of the four images of Ādinātha (Ṛishabhanātha) in the hoard, one depicts the pontiff in the *khaḍgāsana* and the rest three showing him as seated in *padmāsana* 'cross legged meditative posture'. The standing Ādinātha (Pl. 1) may easily be recognized by the locks of hair falling on his shoulders. He also bears a topknot on the head. Standing on a lotus seat (*padma-pīṭha*), he wears a *dhotī* 'lower garment' also. Hanging earlobes, sturdy chest, long arms hanging with palms turned inwards, thick lower lip and prominent nose are the noteworthy features.

The image is solid cast and has been treated chemically. The bluish brown patina is clearly seen all over it and indicates excessive iron content. As such, it is quite a heavy piece. There is a latch with a hole at the back for inserting the nail of the halo or the triple umbrella. The lower legs of the pedestal at the back are slightly broken. There is a small single line inscription on the pedestal telling us that this image belonged to Vimala: *(Vasu)-putra-Vimalasya* 'of Vimala, son of Vasu'. The image is 27.5 cm in height and 10.5 cm wide at the feet of the pedestal.

Most beautiful of the *padmāsana* images of Ādinātha is the one (Pl. 2a) measuring 18.5 cm in height and 10.8 cm in width, having a fair amount of copper content and in a very good state of preservation. The pontiff is shown as seated in *padmāsana* with an oblong beaded aureole behind the head. The matted locks of the tīrthaṅkara are taken backwards, rolled in the form of a pod or *ushṇīsha* and fall on the shoulders from behind the head in a wavy way. The pod on the head seems to have been adorned in front by a beaded jewel. The Jina has a prominent and broad forehead, long quasi-closed eyes, sturdy nose, long drawn mouth, thick lower lip, round chin, oval face and hanging earlobes. The elongate body with long arms is carved very exquisitely. The muscles of the chest are quite prominent. The Jina is seated on a lotus placed upon the pedestal. The crossbar of the back-slab is supported by pillars whose outer sides are also beaded. The corners between the halo and the crossbar are occupied by stylized crocodile heads. The cognizance bull is shown couchant to left on the pedestal. Before the bull is a human figure in profile in the kneeling posture. Behind him are shown two human figures seated in *añjali-mudrā* (gesture of veneration and worship in which the palms are joined together) in two registers. Similar figures are shown at the back of the bull on the sides and at the back of the pedestal as well as on the pillars of the back seat. The topmost figure on the proper right hand side pillar is, however, shown with extended arms holding some unidentified objects. The total number of these figures in adoration is thirty-nine. All are in *padmāsana* and are executed rather crudely. They may represent twelve Chakravartins, nine Vāsudevas, nine Baladevas and nine Prati-Vāsudevas (Pls. 2b-e). The palms and soles of the tīrthaṅkara show pellets (*chakras*).

The third image of Ādinātha, seated in *padmāsana* on a cushioned seat, shows the usual feature of locks of hair falling on the shoulders of the pontiff. The hair are beautifully combed and parted in the centre and the *ushṇīsha* has been shown on the top (Pl. 3). The hair falling on the shoulders are in the form of curled multiple locks. The open eyes, prominent eyebrows, sturdy nose, thick lips, rounded chin and plump cheeks provide the oval face a uniqueness of its own. There is a big oblong hole behind the head. Two small holes in the halo on the upper right and a looped hole on the left were probably meant for some attachment covering a part of the wide halo above the head of the tīrthaṅkara. The halo is bedecked by four conch-like curled attachments on the fringe and by a double one (forming the upper part of the *śrīvatsa* 'an auspicious symbol') at the top. The *prabhā-chakra* 'aureole' is placed on the crossbar of the back seat. To provide support to the crossbar, *vyāla* 'griffin' figures have been provided in the form of brackets. A male figure has survived on the proper right hand side of the Jina while the other on the left is gone. This male wears a necklace, *valayas* 'bangles', *dhotī* 'nether garment', etc. and holds an unidentified object (looking like a fish) in his *pralamba* 'hanging' left hand while the suspended right hand holds the hem of the undergarment. The figure is very crudely executed. A small hole on the facet of the pedestal indicates that the cognizance bull was attached here. It is a fairly preserved image with a fair amount of copper content. It is 21.0 cm high and 13.5 cm in breadth.

The fourth figure of Ādinātha shows the pontiff seated in *padmāsana* on a *siṃhāsana* 'lion throne' the frontal side of which carries the small depictions of outgoing lions with an eight-fellied *chakra* 'discus' in the centre (Pl. 4). In the upper part of the front of the pedestal are shown eight roundish heads representing the *grahas* 'planetary divinities'. There is a leaf-shaped gloriole behind the head of the tīrthaṅkara. Lozenge-shaped *śrīvatsa* on the chest is very clear though the image is badly corroded. *Ushṇīsha* with topknot, wide open eyes, prominent eyebrows, sturdy nose, thick lips, fleshy cheeks and lock of hair falling on the shoulders are the usual features. There are traces of the sandal paste all over the image indicating that it was under worship before being buried. A part of the back-slab on the right has been broken. The corrosion indicates substantial amount of iron content. There are traces of an inscription at the back which, however, cannot be deciphered because of the corrosion.

Mallinātha

One bronze (Pl. 5), 24 cm in height and 13 cm in width, is very interesting as it is executed in a different style. It shows the tīrthaṅkara seated in *padmāsana* on a lotus seat with a beautiful winding vine forming an elliptical back-slab with three curved branches touching and supporting the inner periphery of the ellipse to which are welded miniature figures of the *navagrahas* 'nine planetary divinities' shown as seated in different postures but to be definitely recognized by Rāhu offering oblation on the proper left hand side of the tīrthaṅkara. Because of excessive corrosion, the attributes in the hands of the planetary divinities and other details cannot be made out properly. The triple umbrella surmounts the elliptical back-slab. Of great interest, however, is the pedestal which shows two elephants in profile touching from above a vase placed in the centre with their stretched trunks. In Jaina images, a *chakra* is flanked by two deer, or by two lions or by two cognizances of the Jinas.[1] If the elephants are taken as the cognizances, then the tīrthaṅkara may be recognized as Ajitanātha, but if the water-jar in the

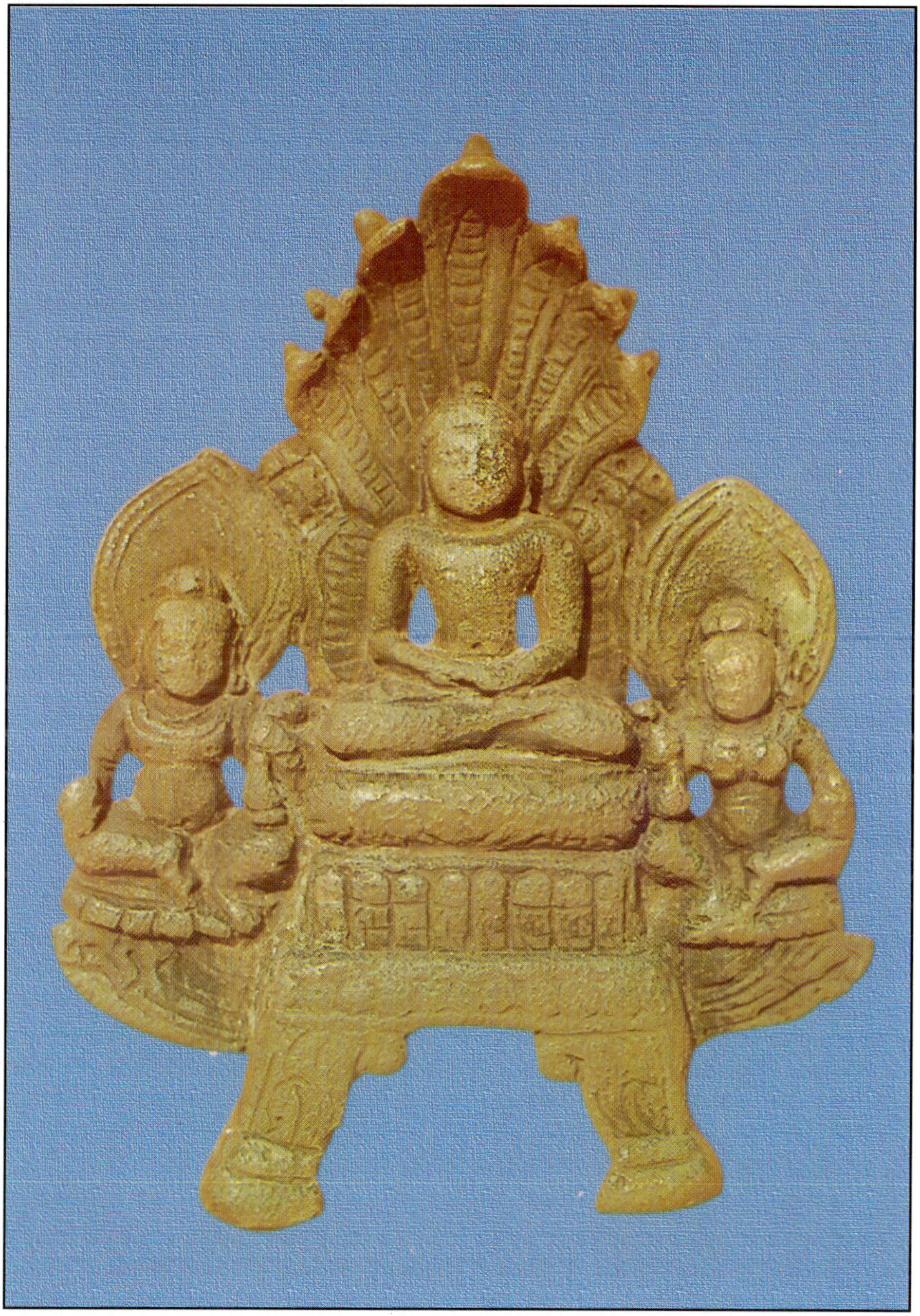

Pl. 16. *Padmāsana* Pārśvanātha with Sarvānubhūti and Ambikā

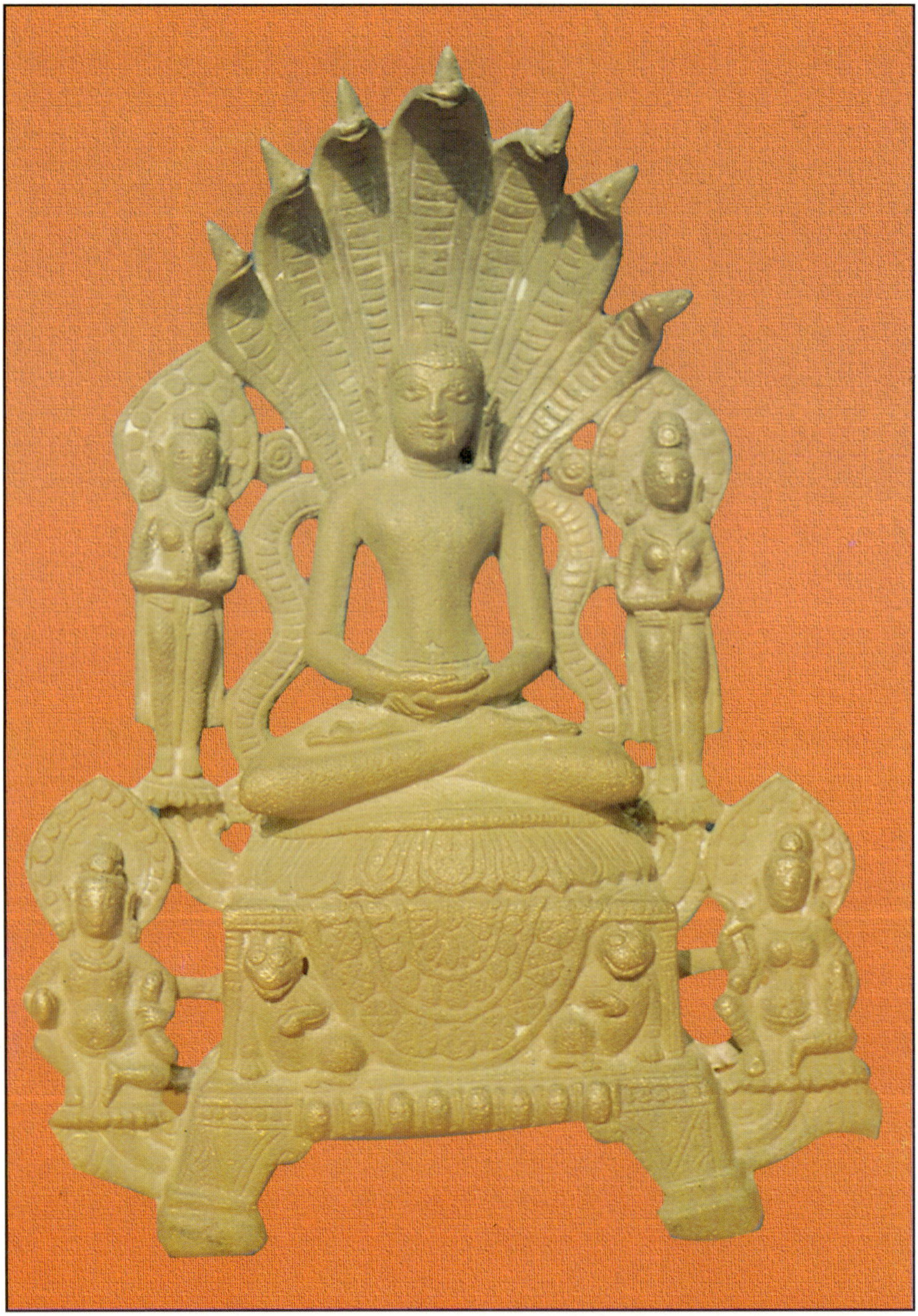

Pl. 17

Pls. 17-18. *Padmāsana* Pārśvanātha with serpent-hooded attendants, Sarvānubhūti and Ambikā

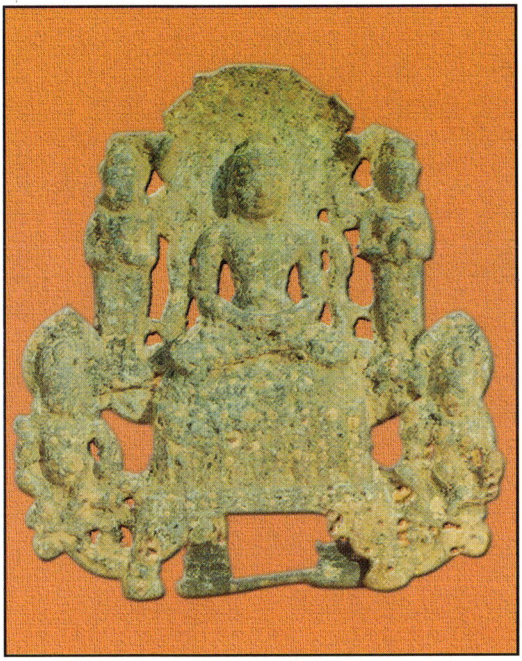

Pl. 18

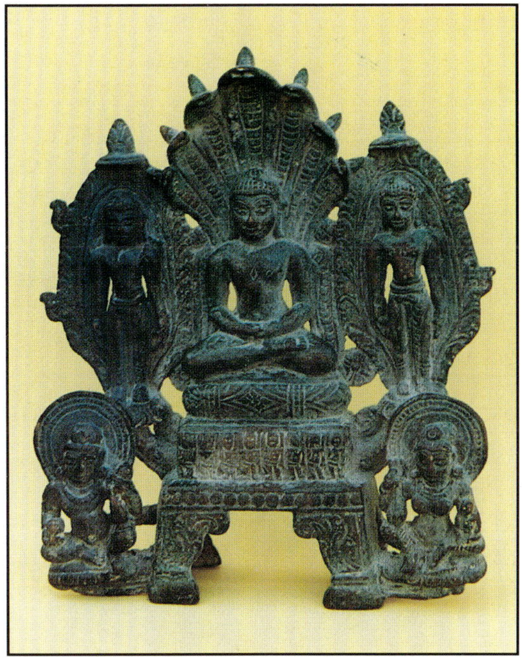

Pl. 19a. *Tri-tīrthikā* of Pārśvanātha

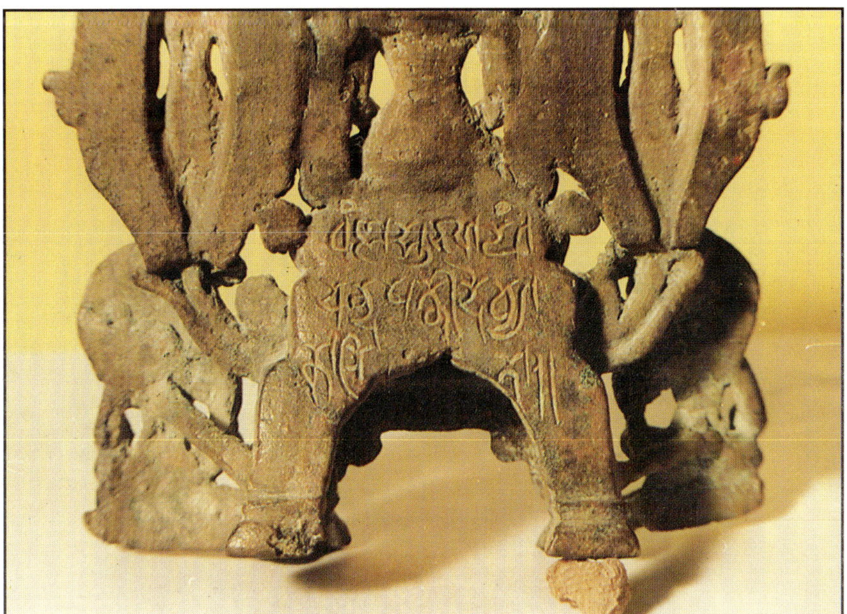

Pl. 19b. Inscription at the back

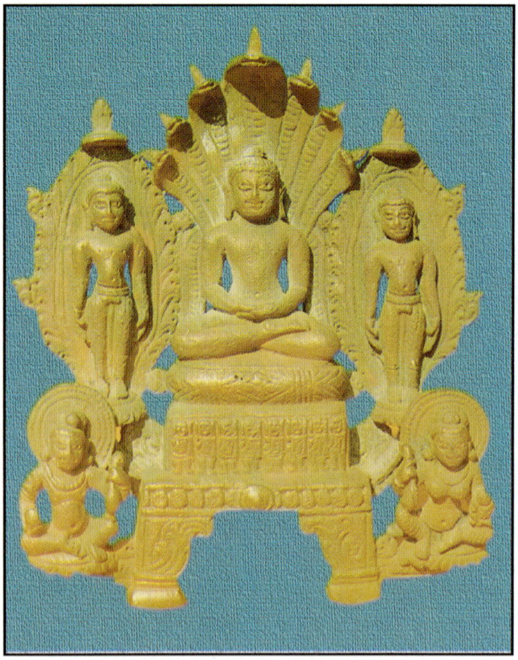

Pl. 20a. *Tri-tīrthikā* of Pārśvanātha

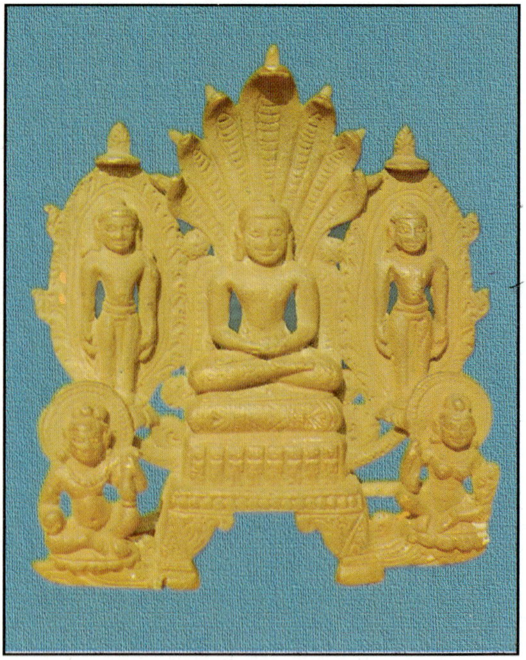

Pl. 21. *Tri-tīrthikā* of Pārśvanātha

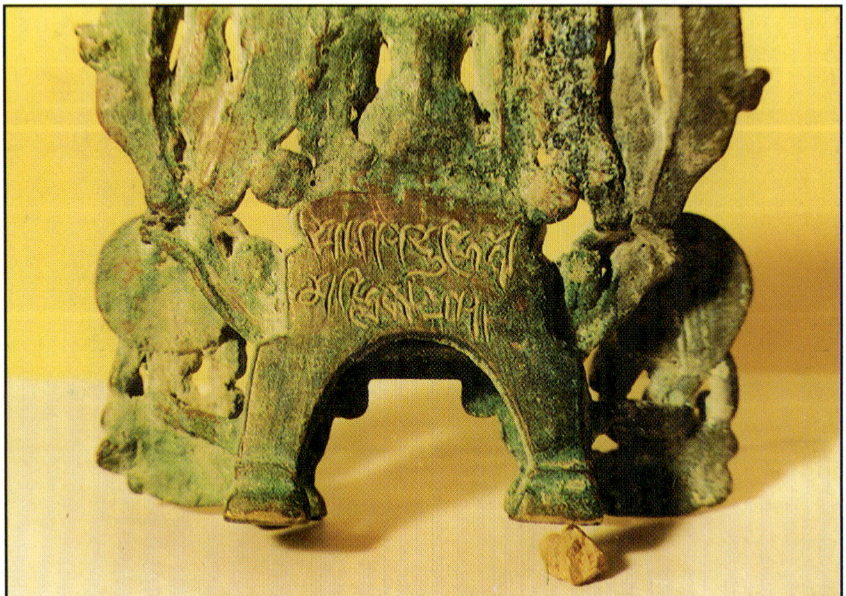

Pl. 20b. Inscription at the back

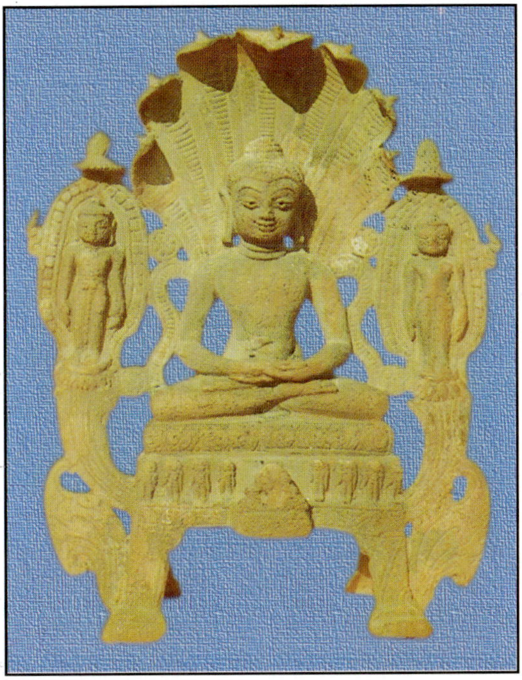

Pl. 22. *Tri-tīrthikā* of Pārśvanātha

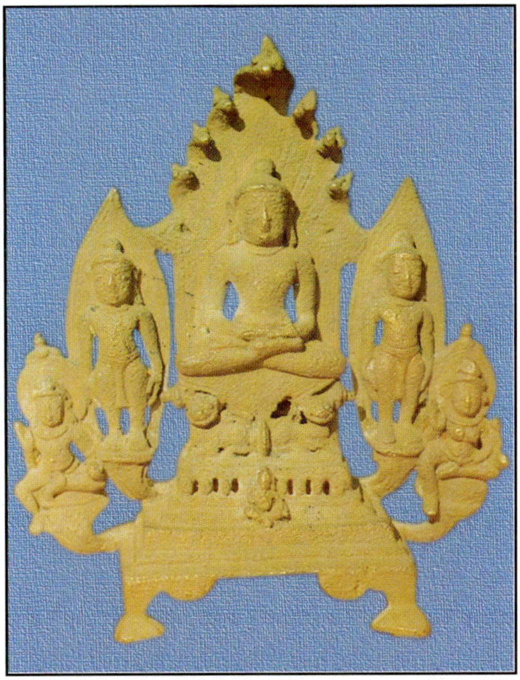

Pl. 24. *Tri-tīrthikā* of Pārśvanātha (with locks falling on the pontiff's shoulders)

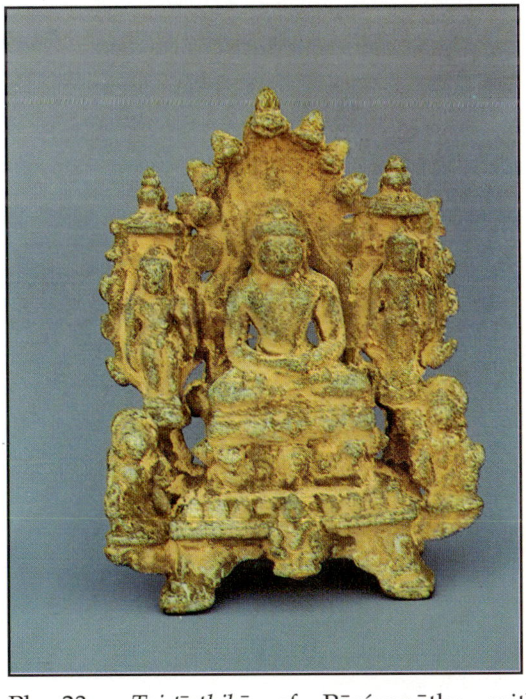

Pl. 23a. *Tri-tīrthikā* of Pārśvanātha with Sarvānubhūti and Ambikā (before treatment)

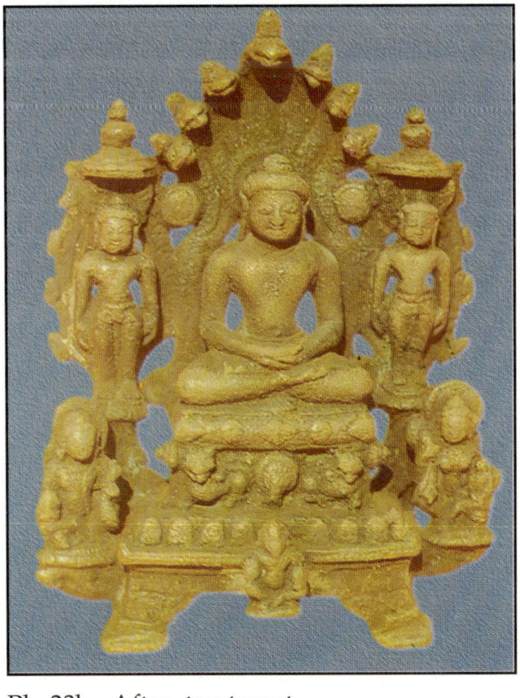

Pl. 23b. After treatment

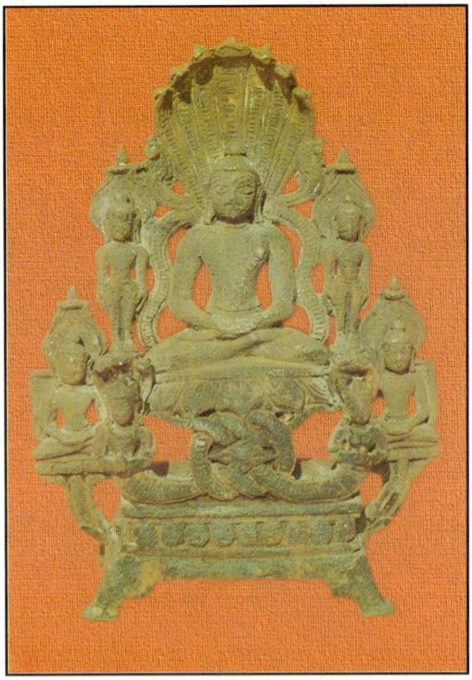

Pl. 25

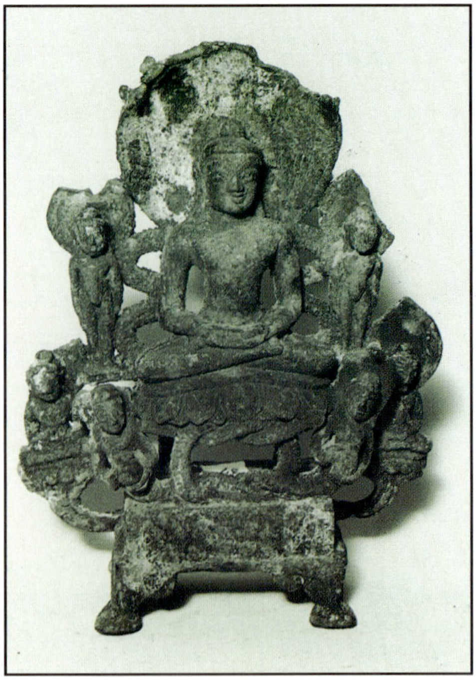

Pl. 26

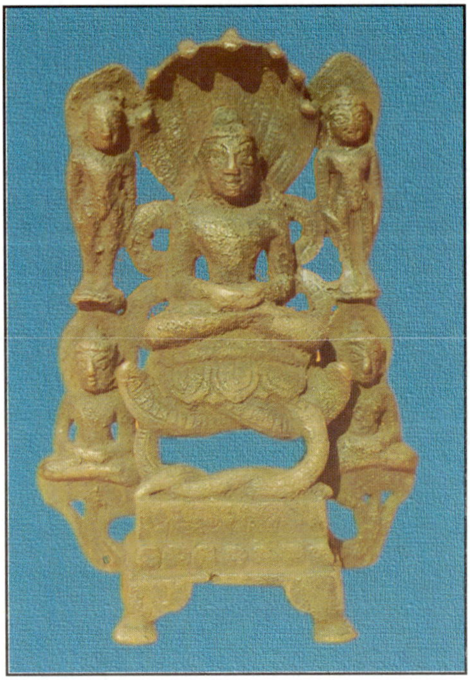

Pl. 27

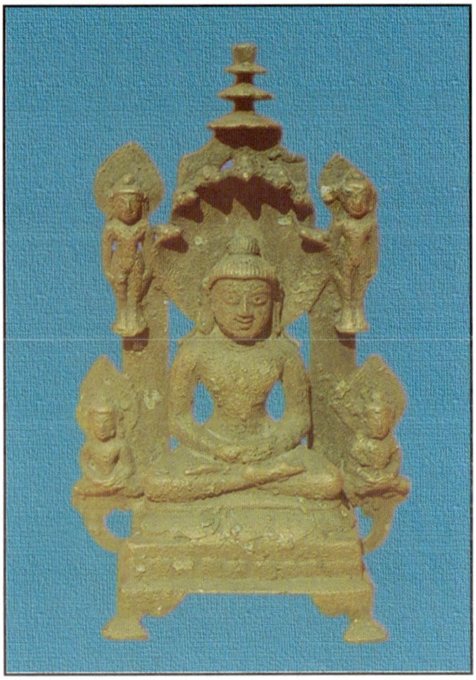

Pl. 28

Pls. 25-28. *Pañcha-tīrthikās* of Pārśvanātha

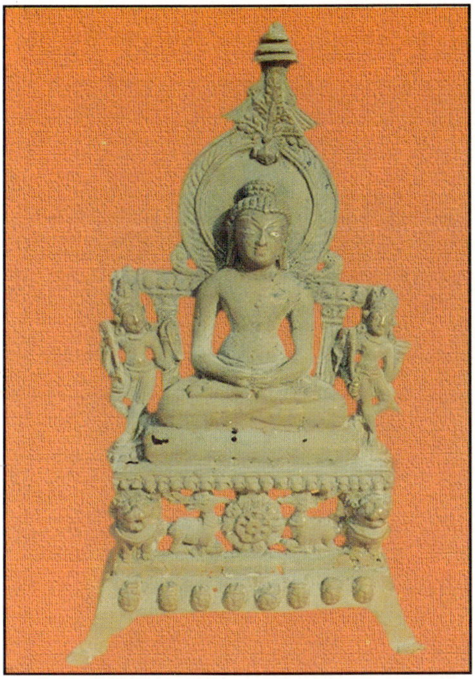

Pl. 29. Mahāvīra

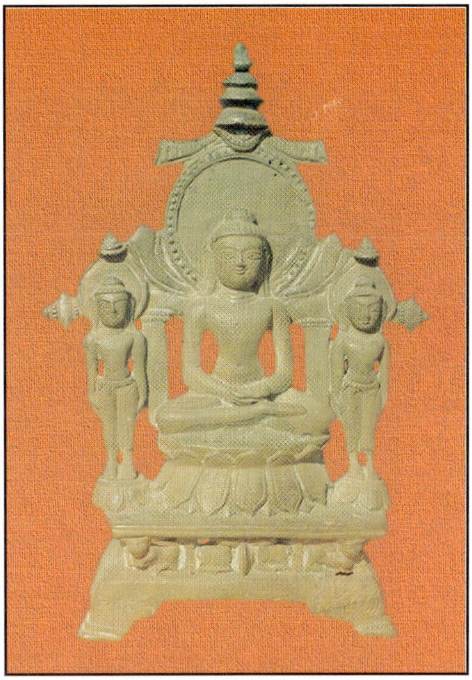

Pl. 30. *Tri-tīrthikā* of Mahāvīra

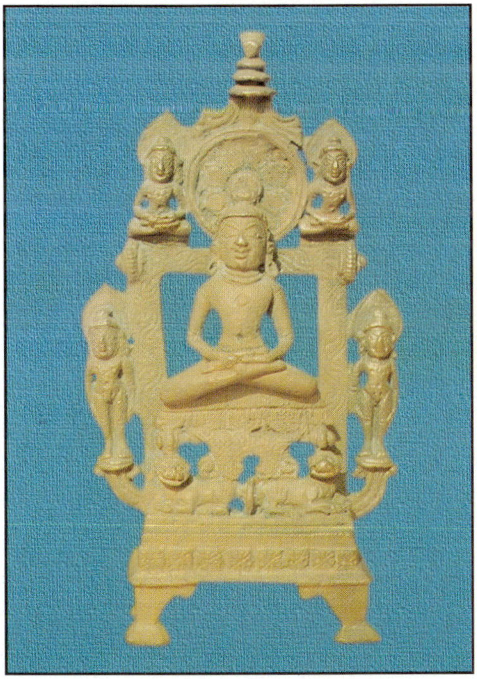

Pl. 31

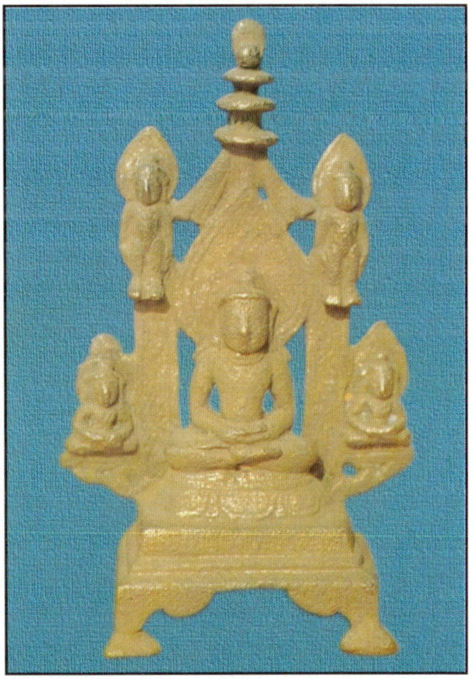

Pl. 32

Pls. 31-32. *Pañcha-tīrthikās* of Mahāvīra

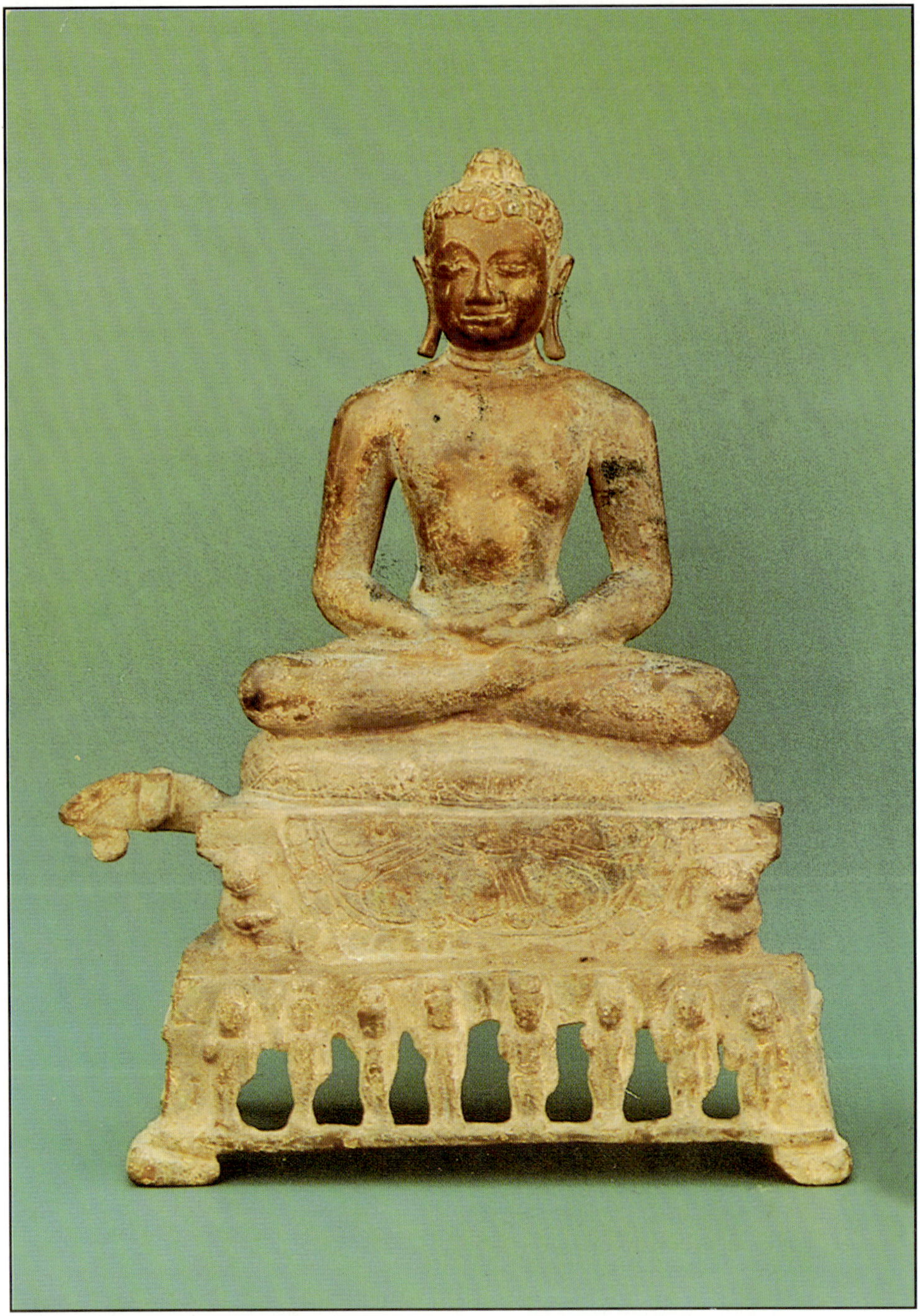

Pl. 33. Mahāvīra (incomplete)

centre is taken as the cognizance the Jina is Mallinātha. The depiction of the water-jar flanked by elephants, however, is a unique feature and has got neither any precedence nor any repetition. In the absence of the yaksha and yakshī figures, the problem of proper identification gets more difficult.

Very interesting, however, is another image (Pl. 6) depicting the tīrthaṅkara seated in *padmāsana* on an inverted lotus flanked by a female fly-whisker on either side. There is an oblong gloriole behind the head and an umbrella above. What is most remarkable is that the tīrthaṅkara is a female with round breasts. As such, the figure may be recognized as that of Mallinātha.[2] The planetary divinities, eight in number, are shown on the pedestal. Seven of them are in the standing posture, beginning with Sūrya on the left, and one on the extreme right is Rāhu (with only the upper half bust) offering oblation. The image was badly corroded but treated subsequently. Though images of Malli in female form are known in stone,[3] none in bronze is known so far. The *Nāyādhammakahāo*, one of the Aṅga texts of the Jaina canon and datable to the Gupta period, refers to a life-size golden image of the princess Malli, who later became a tīrthaṅkara.[4] No such image, however, has been discovered from anywhere so far. This, thus, is the first bronze image of female Mallinātha to come to light. It measures 17 X 12 cm.

Chandraprabha

The Hansi hoard contains two images of Chandraprabha, the eighth tīrthaṅkara. One of these is executed very exquisitely (Pl. 7a). The Jina is seated in *padmāsana* on a lotus seat below which is a *chakra* in the centre with two lions in profile seated on their haunches, having their backs towards the discus. The lions are almost enface and have one of their paw raised up. Crescent, the cognizance of the Jina, may be seen on the pedestal. Chandraprabha is shown as *kambu-grīva* 'with conch-like neck', having a wig-like coiffure of schematic curls with topknot, bow-like eyebrows, long eyes almost closed in concentration, sharp nose, thick lips and plump cheeks. An interesting feature of the image is the depiction of locks falling on the shoulders as in the images of Ādinātha. This feature has been noticed in some other images also.[5] The Jina has a lozenge-shaped *śrīvatsa* mark on the chest. This mark is segmented by a cross in it. Two fly-whiskers standing on lotus flowers emanating from the back of the pedestal flank the Jina. The figures are adorned beautifully and have leaf-shaped halos. On the crossbar flanking the eight-petalled lotus gloriole stand two Jinas in *khaḍgāsana* with laceolate *śiraśchakras* 'nimbuses'. The space between the lotus-petalled halo of Chandraprabha and the crossbar is filled by half-diamond pattern. The triple umbrella crowns the round *prabhā-chakra* of the tīrthaṅkara. No *tri-tīrthikā* of Chandraprabha in metal is known so far. This, thus, is a unique piece.

The image has sufficient copper content, which has given it its hue. At the back of the image (Pl. 7b) is an inscription which may tentatively be read as *Sukhadeva-suta Ha...* '(of) Ha..., son of Sukhadeva'. Palaeographically, it may be paced in *circa* eighth century AD. The image is 23.5 cm in height and 14.3 cm in width.

The second figure of Chandraprabha (Pl. 8) is a smaller one measuring 9.2 cm in height and 7.2 cm in width. The tīrthaṅkara is seated in *padmāsana* on an inverted lotus placed on the throne which carries a crescent on its front with four very crudely carved standing figures of the planetary divinities on either side. The tīrthaṅkara has a round face with *ushṇīsha* and top-knot, long earlobes, arched eyebrows, thick lips, thick squatted nose and wide open eyes having pricked eyeballs. The lozenge-shaped *śrīvatsa* on the chest has been shown very prominently. The halo bears engraved decorations. At the apex is the umbrella. The heads of the attendant figures are proportionately larger and they wear *dhotīs* which are marked by engraved folds. They stand in *añjali-mudrā*. The back of the image is plain.

Pārśvanātha

As noted above, the Hansi hoard contains twenty images of Pārśvanātha, the largest number for any tīrthaṅkara, which surely furnish evidence of the great popularity of this tīrthaṅkara. Some of these images may be ranked as the best known specimens and may well be compared with the images of the Akota hoard.[6] There are as many as eight independent figures of Pārśvanātha, seven *tri-tīrthikās* and five *pañcha-tīrthikās* of Pārśvanātha in the hoard. At least two fragmentary figures, one of the pontiff himself and one each of the detached Dharaṇendra and Padmāvatī, may also be added to this list though their extant remains do not enable us to identify them exactly whether they were the independent figures or *tri-tīrthikās* or *pañcha-tīrthikās*.

In one of the well preserved images (Pl. 9) Pārśvanātha is shown as seated on a lotus seat in *padmāsana* under the canopy of a seven-hooded snake, attended by Dharaṇendra and his queen Padmāvatī, both seated in *lalitāsana* (sitting posture of ease with one leg placed on the ground and the other folded on the seat) with folded hands and canopied by unicephalic snakes. The Jina bears a lozenge-shaped *śrīvatsa* on the chest. Eight standing figures of the planetary divinities (without Rāhu) are depicted on the pedestal. The figures are worn out beyond recognition. Such a depiction of the *grahas* exists on many other images of the hoard as we have seen above. A few specimens of Akota bronzes also show this feature.[7]

The yaksha and yakshī have been attached to the coils of the serpent with connecting rods. Probably the Jina on the pedestal was cast in one mould, the coiled seven-hooded serpent in another and the yaksha and yakshī also in separate moulds. Later they were welded together.[8] The image is 16.5 cm in height and 13.2 cm in width.

Another image (Pl. 10), though badly broken, shows the yaksha and yakshī hooded by unicephalic serpents emanating from the pedestal. They are shown with folded hands. On the pedestal are depicted eight roundels indicating the planetary divinities (without Rāhu). In yet another figure, which is similar in conception and composition but very badly corroded, the yaksha and yakshī are shown as standing in *añjali-mudrā* under the hoods of single-headed snakes on the lotus flowers emanating from the two sides of the pedestal of the pontiff (Pl. 11). Another figure (Pl. 12) shows *padmāsana* Pārśva under the canopy of seven-hooded snake flanked by Dharaṇendra and Padmāvatī, both having snake canopies, standing on lotus *pīṭhas* 'moulded bases' emanating from behind the pedestal, and with eight of the planetary divinities on the pedestal. The lozenge-shaped *śrīvatsa* may also be seen on the chest of the tīrthaṅkara. The figure measures 15.3 X 10.0 cm and is plain at the back. After treatment it has come out to be a beautiful image betraying well-modelled and proportionate figures. A squatish hollow cast image showing holes because of corrosion depicts the pontiff in *padmāsana* flanked by yaksha Sarvānubhūti and yakshī Ambikā seated in *lalitāsana* on lotus flowers emanating from the back of the pedestal (Pl. 13). Sarvānubhūti holds a *nakulaka* 'mongoose purse' in his left hand while the right is held in protection giving posture. Ambikā holds an *āmra-lumbī* 'mango-bunch' in her right hand and supports a child with the left. The yaksha has a leaf-shaped halo with a beaded border. The halo behind the head of Ambikā is broken and the extant part is too corroded to reveal the details of decoration. Projecting at the centre of the pedestal is a semicircular lotus with two deer and a discus on a pillar in the middle. The back is plain. The image is 18.5 cm in height and 19.0 cm in width.

Another image of Pārśva (Pl. 14), badly corroded and broken has also lost the upper parts of the hoods canopying Pārśva like the preceding example. It is not flanked by the female figures with folded hands but shows similarly disposed yaksha and yakshī figures of Sarvānubhūti and Ambikā seated in *lalitāsana* on lotus flowers emanating from the back of the pedestal of the Jina and having leaf-shaped halos behind their heads. Another similar bronze (Pl. 15), but a complete one, shows a semicircular projection in the centre of the pedestal depicting the wheel surmounted on a pillar flanked by two deer. This bronze figure still carries traces of the sandal paste on it clearly indicating that it was under worship at the time of the burial. One of the most graceful figures of Pārśvanātha (Pl. 16), however, depicts the pontiff seated on a lotus cushion in *padmāsana* with hands placed one over the other in the lap, having a *śrāvatsa* mark on the chest and canopied by the seven-hooded serpent. Eight standing stylized planetary divinities stand on the pedestal with a register of rosettes below. Yaksha Sarvānubhūti holding an unidentified object in the right hand and a *nakulaka* in the left sits in *ardhparyaṅkāsana* on a lotus seat. He has a topknot on the head and wears *karṇa-kuṇḍalas* 'earrings', *keyūras* 'armlets' and perhaps wristlets too. There is a laceolate gloriole with a beaded border enclosed in two lines behind the head. Ambikā sits almost symmetrically on the other side holding an *āmra-lumbī* in the right hand and supporting a diminutive figure of a child on the left knee with the other hand. With its exquisite carving, proportionate figures, graceful curves and contours and harmonious composition, it may be classed amongst the best figures in the lot.

One of the most beautifully executed image (Pl. 17), measuring 18.5 X 14.0 cm, depicts the elongated figure of Pārśva seated in *padmāsana* under the canopy of the seven-hooded snake flanked on either side by a female figure in *añjali-mudrā* with a leaf-shaped aureole behind the head. The front of the pedestal has the circular covering with an outgoing lion on either side. Yaksha Kuberaka (Sarvānubhūti) and yakshī Ambikā are depicted on the two sides of the pedestal seated in *lalitāsana* and with leaf-shaped halos. On the lower register of the pedestal are shown eight rounded figures of the *grahas*. There seem to be traces of an inscription at the back but it has been almost completely concealed by the heavy corrosion blackish in colour. Another piece (Pl. 18) shows similarly placed figures but with standing *navagrahas* on the pedestal. It is so heavily corroded that other details cannot be made out clearly. Also the hoods of the serpent above the head of the pontiff and the back legs of the pedestal are broken.

Tri-tīrthikās of Pārśvanātha

The hoard contains seven *tri-tīrthikās* of Pārśvanātha. All of them are beautiful pieces vying with the best-known images of this type. One of the best preserved of these *tri-tīrthikās* (Pl. 19a) shows Pārśvanātha seated on an embroidered cushion in *padmāsana* under the canopy of a seven-hooded snake. The Jina with beatitudinous smiling face, quasi-closed eyes, long pointed nose, thick lower lip, round cheeks and chin, round shoulders, slender waist and well proportioned limbs has been executed very exquisitely. The standing Jinas on his sides share the physical features of Pārśva and have oblong flamboyant halos. The one on the proper right hand side of Pārśvanātha is Ādinātha as can be recognized from the locks of hair falling on his shoulders. The corresponding left Jina cannot be identified with certainty but may have been Mahāvīra. Both the flanking Jinas wear *dhotīs*. Just below the cushion seat of Pārśvanātha is carved eight standing figures of the planets. The lower band shows eleven rosettes. To the feet of the pedestal are attached the figures of Sarvānubhūti and Ambikā on the proper right and left sides respectively. They sit in *ardha-paryaṅkāsana* on the lotus seats. Both wear ear ornaments, *ekāvalis*, *keyūrus*, *valayas* 'bangles' and undergarments. The coiffures are also similar. The hair is combed backwards and tied in a large bun adorned in front with a jewel. They have circular halos bearing beaded design between lined circles. The yaksha is slightly pot-bellied and holds a citron in his right hand and a money-bag in his left. The yakshī holds an *āmra-lumbī* in her right hand and supports the child seated on her left leg with the corresponding hand.

The image has retained its coppery look and is an excellent specimen of the art of the region. It can well be compared with the *tri-tīrthikā* of Pārśvanātha from Akota.[9] It bears an inscription on the back (Pl. 19b) which reads *Vallasukhāyā[ḥ] Chandra-patnī-Devyā kāritā*, i.e. (This image was) caused to be made by Devī, the wife of Chandra, hailing from Vallasukhā.[10] Palaeography suggests *circa* seventh-eighth century as the date of the image. It measures 14 X 12 cm.

This image was cast in six different pieces: Pārśvanātha on the pedestal, the serpent, the two standing Jinas, the yaksha and the yakshī.

These pieces were then welded to give this image its present shape.

Almost exactly similar is another piece with the inscription *Sāgara-duhitā Mahlikāyā[ḥ]* 'of Mahlikā, daughter of Sāgara' at the back datable to the same period (Pls. 20a & b). The two images are so similar that they seem to have been cast and carved by the same artist. The only difference between them is that the latter has turned bluish green because of different contents of the alloy from which it was prepared. This indicates that the artists used to vary the metal contents of the alloy according to the requirements of the customers to match their pockets. The piece measures 14.3 X 12.6 cm. A third piece of the same size and make (Pl. 21) bears a two line inscription at the back which reads *Sāgara-patnī Lakhukāyā[ḥ]* 'of Lakhukā, wife of Sāgara'. The name of Sāgara is common to this and the preceding piece. Both the wife of Sāgara and his daughter seem to have got similar *tri-tīrthikās* of Pārśvanātha prepared, probably from the same artist. This is borne out by their execution as well as palaeography. Before treatment, it bore traces of sandal paste on it. In still another similar piece, measuring 14.8 X 13.5 cm, which has turned blackish green with corrosion, the inscription at the back is not clearly visible and only the last word *śrāvakaḥ* 'lay disciple' can be made out.

A *tri-tīrthikā*, measuring 19.0 X 15.5 cm, shows Pārśvanātha seated in *padmāsana* under seven-hooded snake-canopy, flanked on either side by Jinas in *khaḍgāsana* standing on full blown lotus flowers with beaded bordered oblong halos capped by umbrellas (Pl. 22). The pedestal bears frontally standing eight human figures of the *grahas* and a triangular projecting piece showing two deer and a *chakra* on a pillar between them. Simple in conception this is a highly aesthetic piece in execution. Originally, this image too bore a layer of sandal paste at places. There is another similar image (Pl. 23a) of slightly smaller dimensions (13.5 X 10.8 cm). It shows eight round dots representing the eight *grahas* on the pedestal and the deer and *chakra* replaced by the seated miniature figure of bearded Brahmā in *sukhāsana*,[11] with the yaksha Nakulaka (Sarvānubhūti) and yakshī Ambikā attached to the pedestal. After treatment it has turned out to be a very beautiful image (Pl. 23b).

The last of the *tri-tīrthikās* (Pl. 24) is similar in conception and measures 14.7 cm in height and 13.0 cm in width. Though only slightly bigger than the preceding piece, it gives the impression of an elongate image probably because of the leaf-shaped full halos behind the flanking Jinas in *kāyotsarga*. Another notable feature is the locks of hair falling on the shoulders of Pārśvanātha like that of Ādinātha. Bearded and pot-bellied Bṛihaspati here occupies a slightly higher place in the middle of the pedestal. Corrosion has badly affected this image which after treatment shows a fair amount of copper content.

Pañcha-tīrthikās of Pārśvanātha

Of the five *pañcha-tīrthikās* of Pārśva in the Hansi hoard, the best preserved one (Pl. 25) shows the tīrthaṅkara seated in *padmāsana* on an inverted lotus which is placed on the coils of the intertwined tails of a snake couple whose upper halves are human and are shown in *añjali-mudrā,* canopied by three hoods. The front face of the pedestal bears in a row nine round human heads representing the *navagrahas.* Two lotuses emanate from the back of the pedestal on which are shown two *padmāsana* Jinas having square back-slabs and round halos capped by umbrellas. Two Jinas have been shown in *khaḍgāsana* almost parallel to the main figure. There seems to have been an inscription at the back but because of the heavy corrosion it is not possible to read it. The blackish core at the back and the greenish patina indicate more of iron content. The figure of Pārśvanātha is quite proportionate bearing a topknot. The image measures 18.8 X 15.0 cm.

Another *pañcha-tīrthikā* (Pl. 26) is similar in conception though very badly corroded. Pārśvanātha sits on the inverted lotus placed on the coils of a *nāga* 'serpent' and *nāgī* 'she-serpent' who are hybrid in nature having human busts and canopied by one-hooded snake. They hold water-vessels in their hands. This is an interesting feature. The hoods of the cobra which canopy the tīrthaṅkara are damaged on the top right. The piece measures 14.7 X 13.0 cm. Like other images it has also been cast in different pieces.

A simple *pañcha-tīrthikā* (Pl. 27) shows Pārśva seated in *padmāsana* on an inverted lotus placed on the coils of the zoomorphic snakes. The Jina is canopied as usual by the seven-hooded snake but shows the locks falling on the shoulders like Ādinātha. From either side of the pedestal spring two lotus stalks showing two miniature Jinas in *padmāsana* having plain halos. Two sky-clad Jinas stand in *kāyotsarga*, attached to the coils of the snake at the back of Pārśvanātha. They have plain pointed-top halos. The pedestal contains only seven round heads of the astral divinities and both Rāhu and Ketu are absent. The image contains sufficient copper content but the corrosion has badly affected the image. It has now been treated. It is an important piece belonging to the Digambaras as indicated by sky-clad Jinas. Most of the images described above show the undergarments worn by additional Jina figures. Evidently, the two sects had very harmonious relations at Hansi.

Another *pañcha-tīrthikā* (Pl. 28) depicts Pārśvanātha seated on a lotus seat on the throne flanked by two *padmāsana* and two *kāyotsarga* Jinas, all having plain pointed-top halos. There is, however, a triple umbrella shown above the seven hoods of the serpent canopying Pārśva. The pontiff bears a beautiful topknot and the locks of hair are shown as falling on his shoulders. The prominent lozenge-shaped *śrīvatsa* is also clearly visible on the chest. Nine roundels on the pedestal represent the *navagrahas*. The figure measures 18 X 11 cm. A small *pañcha-tīrthikā* of 12.5 X 8.0 cm also shares most of the features of the preceding piece but is very badly corroded.

A broken piece shows the figure of Pārśva seated in *padmāsana* with hybrid *nāga-nāgī* figures in *añjali-mudrā* and canopied by single hooded snakes springing outwards from the pedestal. A detached piece represents a small *padmāsana* figure having a multi-hooded snake canopying him but only two of the hoods have survived.

Mahāvīra

Five images in the hoard may be identified as those of Mahāvīra, the last tīrthaṅkara. Very elegant is an image (Pl. 29) which shows the tīrthaṅkara seated in *padmāsana* flanked by male fly-whiskers. Mahāvīra has a well-proportioned body with rounded shoulders, long arms folded in the lap with palms placed one over the other. The *ushṇīsha* with a topknot, long earlobes, quasi-closed elongate eyes, bow-like eyebrows, thick lower lip, round chin, plump cheeks and oval face are noteworthy features. The *śrīvatsa* on the chest is also clear. The halo behind the head is plain in the centre but has a broad border marked with oblique flame-like lined decorations, the top being bedecked by a potted tree having five branches, the central one rising vertically, and the apex capped by the triple umbrella. The fly-whiskers stand gracefully in *tribhaṅga* 'triple flexion', wearing bejewelled crowns, earrings, *ekāvalis*, bracelets, undergarments, etc., holding the fly-whisks in their right hands and unidentified objects in their left hands. They stand cross-legged with one foot placed on a lotus below. The pedestal shows a beautiful *chakra* in the centre flanked by inward looking deer in profile with enface lions at the corners. Below on the pedestal are depicted eight of the *navagrahas* in the form of round heads. The sandal paste in the left eye of the tīrthaṅkara even after its chemical treatment indicates the long time for which it was under worship before its deposition. As a result of the removal of the thick corrosion, holes have been caused in the thin sheet from which it seems to have been hollow cast. It measures 24.7 cm in height and 15.0 cm in width.

A *tri-tīrthikā* of Mahāvīra (Pl. 30) depicts the tīrthaṅkara in *padmāsana* on a double-petalled lotus flanked by *khaḍgāsana* Jinas, standing on lotus flowers and wearing *dhotīs*. The main figure has a round halo with beaded border capped by *chhattrāvali* and the standing figures too have plain pointed-top glorioles with triple umbrellas. The pedestal bears a disc in profile in the centre between two deer, and two lions have been shown as moving outwards with faces turned to front. On the pedestal is an inscription also of which only *sivaṭa* in the beginning and *tya* at the end are decipherable. It is a carefully executed image of great aesthetic value belonging to the Śvetāmbara sect as indicated by the undergarments worn by the *khaḍgāsana* Jinas flanking the main figure. It measures 24 X 17 cm.

A *pañcha-tīrthikā* of Mahāvīra (Pl. 31) shows the tīrthaṅkara seated on a double- petalled lotus seat with an eight-petalled round gloriole having a double-lined circular border surmounted by a triple umbrella. Two *padmāsana* miniature Jinas with plain pointed-top halos flank the *prabhā-chakra* of Mahāvīra while two sky-clad *khaḍgāsana* Jinas with similar halos are shown standing on lotuses emanating from the back of the pedestal on the sides. The pedestal carries a wheel in profile between two outward sitting enface lions. There is a prominent *śrīvatsa* on the chest of Mahāvīra who also bears a prominent topknot and long earlobes as if wearing rings. The depiction of the astral deities has been reduced to only a decorative motif on the pedestal. The execution is rather crude though the figure is in a good state of preservation after treatment. It is 15 cm in height and 8 cm in width. This *pañcha-tīrthikā* belongs to the Digambara sect as indicated by nude standing Jina figures which flank the *padmāsana* Mahāvīra. The preceding *tri-tīrthikā* and the present image, thus, provide important evidence of the harmony which prevailed at that time between the two Jaina sects.

Another *pañcha-tīrthikā* (Pl. 32) with central Jina in *padmāsana* flanked by two *khaḍgāsana* and two *padmāsana* tīrthaṅkara, all having leaf-shaped halos, and with a triple umbrella over the central figure, has a simple pedestal without any *lāñchhana* 'cognizance'. The central

Jina, however, is seated on an inverted lotus seat and has locks of hair falling on the shoulders. The feature would indicate that the *pañcha-tīrthikā* belongs to Ādinātha but it is to be noted as we have seen above that at Hansi even other tīrthaṅkaras are shown with such locks. As such, we cannot be sure whether this *pañcha-tīrthikā* belongs to Ādinātha or some other tīrthaṅkara. The image measures 12.5 X 8.0 cm.

A broken but fairly preserved image (Pl. 33) probably also belongs to Mahāvīra as can be made out from the depiction of two outward moving lions on the pedestal. The main figure sits in *padmāsana* and has a muscular body with sturdy features and schematic curls with topknot on the head. Below on the pedestal are depicted eight human figures representing the planets. Another badly corroded *padmāsana* Jina may also be identified as Mahāvīra as the pedestal shows the typical motif of wheel flanked by deer in the centre and outward moving enface lions on the corners. There is a four-petalled bead-rimmed round halo behind the head of the Jina whose physical features recall Gupta art style. Sarvānubhūti holding a *nakulaka* in his left hand and probably a *vīja-puraka* in the right sits in *sukhāsana* on a lotus emanating from the back of the pedestal and has a beaded rimmed pointed-top gloriole behind the head. Ambikā is seated similarly on the other side holding a bunch of mangoes in her right hand and supporting a child seated on her left knee with the other. The front right leg of the pedestal is broken and the top of the aureole too has suffered some damage. After treatment it will surely come out to be an important piece.

The best image amongst the unidentified Jinas (Pl. 34) shows the tīrthaṅkara seated on a cushion in meditation with a beautiful *prabhā-chakra* capped by an umbrella behind and above the head. The halo bears lotus leaf engravings encircled by beads and has a pointed top. The features of the tīrthaṅkara are quite pronounced and the lozenge-shaped *śrīvatsa* on the chest bears a cross-mark. On the pedestal are depicted eight of the *navagrahas* in human form but their execution is very rough. The Jina is flanked by Nakulaka and Ambikā seated on lotus flowers as usual with pointed-top halos. Both of them, however, are shown as wearing jewelled crowns, *karṇa-kuṇḍalas* 'earrings', torques and *dhotīs*. The yaksha holds a *vīja-puraka* in his right hand and money-bag in the left. The yakshī carries the usual attributes. It is a perfectly complete piece and is a beautiful specimen of the metal art of Hansi.

Another aesthetically remarkable image (Pl. 35a) shows the *padamāsana* tīrthaṅkara seated on a lotus seat with a round gloriole bedecked with floral engravings and having a beaded border the top of which is broken slightly and also shows a hole. The yaksha and yakshī are also seated as usual on lotuses emanating from the back of the pedestal but they hold some unidentifiable objects (looking like sugar-cane) in their right hands with left hands on the respective knees. Below the lotus seat of the main figure flanking the stem of the lotus are a man and a woman, the latter holding a child in her left hand. The lowermost register of the pedestal carries crudely carved eight planetary divinities. The image measures 18.0 X 13.5 cm and bears an inscription in two lines at the back of which only a few letters can be made out (Pl. 35b).

The facial features of another unidentified Jina (Pl. 36) are not very distinct because of its worn out condition. The bow-like eyebrows, long contemplating eyes and thick lower lip may, however, be discerned. The Jina has got long hanging earlobes and the stunted neck shows folds simulating a torque.[12] He has a broad chest and a slender waist. The *śrīvatsa* on the chest may also be made out. The shoulders betray some stiffness but the limbs are modelled well. There is a hole above the navel of the Jina and another on the cushion seat. These holes reveal that the image was hollow cast. The pedestal shows very crude eight figures of the planetary divinities. The back-seat and the oval halo seem to have been prepared out of beaten sheets. It bears incised decorations marking a circular beaded halo with flamboyant edges behind the head of the tīrthaṅkara and the pillars supporting the crossbar bedecked with big beads. The pointed pinnacle of the halo has been thickened and projected slightly. It is not definite whether this was done intentionally to give it a serpent-hood like look or is just incidental. The halo also shows a crack. The yaksha and the yakshī have been attached to the image separately. Both have circular halos with borders of big beads. They are Sarvānubhūti and Ambikā, the latter clearly recognizable by the mango-twig and the child she supports in her two hands. After treatment, the image gives brass-like shine. It is 16.0 cm in height and 13.2 cm in width.

It is difficult to identify properly the broken and badly corroded image (Pl. 37) flanked by haloed figures of yaksha and yakshī. The halo of the Jina himself is badly mutilated but what remains gives a semblance of the serpent-hood halo of Pārśvanātha. If so, the image may be that of the penultimate pontiff. But one cannot be sure about it. The yakshī with perhaps a child in her left hand sits on the proper right hand side of the tīrthaṅkara and the yaksha on his left. The yaksha seems to hold a cup in his right hand and a *vīja-puraka* in his left and can, thus, be identified as Kuberaka. The extant height of this piece is 10.5 cm and its breadth is 11.5 cm.

Sarvatobhadrikās

The Hansi hoard contains three *sarvatobhadrikās* of which the best preserved one (Pl. 38a) measures 12.0 cm in height and 9.3 cm in width. Four Jina images are shown on the four facets of a square hollow column on an elegantly moulded pedestal. This, thus, is another good specimen of hollow casting at Hansi.

The Jinas are seated in *padmāsana* on lotus seats and have round halos with a circle of dots enclosed within two-lined circles. The locks have been executed in semi-circular fashion with a topknot above. The pedestal bears floral and beaded mouldings. The figures of the Jinas on the four sides are similar and it is difficult to identify them specifically. The figures have been executed well and bear *śrīvatsa* marks on the chests. The upper corners of the pedestals bear holes for inserting the round shafts, which support the pediment. The detached pediment showed that it contained a *chaitya* 'dormer' window enclosed within half *gavāksha* 'window' motifs and a prominent *chaitya gavāksha* above, surmounted by a massive *āmalaka* 'myrobalan' and the *stūpikā* finial (Pl. 38b). The figure has been treated and gives reddish coppery look. The extant height of the piece is 12.0 cm and width 9.3 cm.

Another *chaumukha* (Pl. 39), though similar, is less decorated. Its superstructure too has got detached. The superstructure consists of a *chaitya*-arch, a massive myrobalan and a vase-shaped finial. It has many holes betraying hollow casting. One of the facets bears traces of an inscription of which only the word *śrāvikā* 'female lay-disciple' can be made out. Probably this *Sarvatobhadrikā* was caused to be made by some female lay worshipper. The *chaumukha* is 21.5 cm high and 8.25 cm wide and bears traces of the sandal paste.

The third piece (Pl. 40a) has lost one leg of the pedestal and has some holes confirming hollow casting. The same tīrthaṅkara seems to have been depicted on all the facets. The Jina figures are robust and squat. In shape, it resembles the first piece. It is badly corroded and measures 15 X 11 cm. Its detached pediment is also available in the hoard (Pls. 41a & b: before and after treatment). It is 10.2 cm in height and 7.5 cm on side. In shape, it is similar to the pediment of the first *chaumukha*.

It may be pointed out that these are the earliest examples of the *Sarvatobhadrikās* in metal known so far.

Parents of the Jina

One image shows the parents of the Jina, both having a hollow oval halo, three-tiered tiara, *ekāvalis*, ear ornaments, *adhovastras* 'lower garment', holding *vīja-purakas* in their right hands and a child each in their left hands (Pl. 42). The stem of a lotus goes up from between the two and is perched by a *padmāsana* Jina bearing a halo and umbrella. On the pedestal are shown seven of the planets in human form, one being obliterated. The depiction of the parents of the Jinas, though known in stone, is rare in metal. This thus is the earliest and so far the only known example in bronze.

Achchhuptā

There are two images of the Mahāvidyā Achchhuptā. The bigger one (Pls. 43 a &b) measures 15.0 cm in height and 6.5 cm in width. She is represented as seated astride on horseback, holding sword and arrow in the normal and extra right hands and bow and shield in the corresponding left hands. She wears a small tiara on her head, circular rings in the ears, *ekāvali* in the neck, *keyūras* on arms, *valayas* on the wrists, the nether garment and full boots. Her hair is combed backwards. She has quasi-closed eyes, prominent nose, small lips and a roundish face. She has full breasts and an attenuated waist. The horse is bedecked with saddle and trappings and has thin long legs. The image has a substantial amount of iron content and bears greenish patina.

The second image (Pls. 44 a & b) is smaller in size, 9.5 X 4.0 cm, and is rather crudely executed. The figure, however, seems to have been solid cast. Achchhuptā, seated cross-legged on horseback to front, has a leaf-shaped halo, wears a bun, *ekāvali*, earrings, bracelets, etc. and holds sword and shield in the back right and left hands while the normal hands seem to support an arrow and bow respectively. The horse is caparisoned and has a hole on the nape and right hand side of the neck. Other details cannot be made out because of heavy corrosion.

Images of Achchhuptā are quite rare both in metal and stone. The Akota hoard contained one piece belonging to the first half of the seventh century AD[13] and none is known so far after that. These metal images of Achcchuptā are, thus, important examples of the depiction of the Mahāvidyā in the early medieval Jaina art of India.

Sarasvatī

The most elegant and the best preserved image of Sarasvatī in the hoard (Pl. 45) represents the goddess standing gracefully in *tribhaṅga* posture on the lotus pedestal holding a lotus in her right hand by its long stalk which rests on the pedestal along with the lower end of her scarf. The scarf is worn over the shoulders and arrangement of its two ends balances the figure. In the *pralamba* left hand, Sarasvatī holds a manuscript. The lotus-petalled bead-bordered halo is damaged above her head. The hair of the goddess of learning is tied in a large chignon on the top of the head adorned in front with *trikūṭaka* 'three-peaked' crown.

The goddess wears *padma-kuṇḍalas* 'lotus rings' in the earlobes and perhaps some other ornaments also on the upper parts of the ears. She also wears an *ekāvali* with a pendant and an *uraḥsūtra* 'breast string'. *Valayas* too may be seen on her wrists. The lower garment is held in position by a double *netra-sūtra* 'waist girdle' whose one end hangs all along the left leg of the goddess who has a square face, rotund breasts and broad hips, the curve to left being accentuated by the *tribhaṅga* posture. Parallel incised lines on the lower garment are clear but the pattern of decoration of the *uttarīya* 'upper garment' is concealed by corrosion. The figure is exquisitely modelled, proportionate and must have been a master- piece in its original form. It can be compared well with the Sarasvatī images from Akota and Vasantgarh.[14] The image in its extant form is 24.0 cm in height and 7.5 cm in width.

One image seems to have been solid cast (Pl. 46). The Mahāvidyā stands gracefully on an inverted lotus placed on a solid pedestal holding the lotus flower in her right hand raised to the level of the shoulder and the manuscript in her *pralamba* left hand. The eyes and eyebrows are incised and the eyeballs are pricked. The nose is slightly damaged. The hair is combed upwards and tied with a bejewelled tiara. The goddess wears thick earrings, torque, bracelets, undergarment secured by a thick rope-like girdle, and a long scarf winding from the back of the goddess and falling down gracefully to the level of the calves from over the arms. Both the *dhotī* and the *uttarīya* bear incised decorations making the folds. There is a pointed-top gloriole behind the head bearing floral decorations. The halo is hollow in the centre behind the head of the Mahāvidyā. The execution is not very meticulous. The image measures 12.5 X 5.0 cm.

The third image of Sarasvatī (Pl. 47) shows the goddess standing in *dvibhaṅga* 'double-flexion' on the lotus seat placed on a legged pedestal. Other details follow the preceding specimen with the difference that the hollow gloriole here bears prick-hole decorations between lined borders. The execution is more crude and the figure looks more stunted though the size of the image is bigger than that of the piece described above. It measures 16.5 X 5.0 cm.

The smallest of the four images of Sarasvatī (Pl. 48) measures 11.2 X 4.0 cm and is very badly corroded. The goddess is depicted as standing to front on the full blown lotus placed on the legged pedestal which also bears inverted petal decoration, now concealed by the corrosion. She has a three-peaked crown on the head and the scarf is smaller in size than what we have seen in the foregoing examples. It hangs only up to the thighs. The manuscript is held in the left hand frontally. The lotus held in the right hand near the shoulder is also full-blown and frontal. The halo is pointed-top but the details are concealed by corrosion. The expression of the goddess, however, seems to be somewhat stiff.

Jaināchārya (?)

The hoard contains an image of a bearded male figure (Pl. 49) seated on a cushion placed on a legged pedestal in *bhadrāsana* 'sitting in European style' wearing a *yoga-paṭṭa* 'yoga-band', holding a rosary in his right hand around the thumb which also touches the pointing finger, and a water-vessel in his left hand placed on his left knee. His matted locks are decorated with jewelled pearl strings and bands. Wide-open eyes have very prominent pricked eyeballs. The nose is very sturdy and he has bow-shaped moustaches. The beard is knotted at the lower end and there is an *akshamālā* 'garland of *aksha* beads' around the neck. The long earlobes bear small earrings. The pointed-top gloriole behind the head is incised with petal designs and has a big beaded border. The beads are enclosed in leaf-shaped lines. The figure has a potbelly and wears a thick multi-stringed sacred thread. *Dhotī* has been marked with incised decorations and wooden sandals in the feet are remarkable. It is difficult to identify the figure definitely. The iconography indicates that the figure may belong to Brahmā but since the hoard does not contain any representation of a Hindu deity there is also the possibility of this figure being that of some prominent Jaina *Āchārya* 'teacher' of Hansi though the presence of the halo with a mortal is an incongruity. The figure, however, is interesting. It measures 8.8 X 6.4 cm.

Pīṭhikā, Loṭās, Śaṅkha and *Arghyā*

As indicated above, the hoard contains some miscellaneous objects also. One *pīṭhikā*, which is 16.0 cm high and 11.5 cm at the feet of the pedestal, is plain at the back and has a socket to support the image at the top (Pl. 50). One *loṭā* (Pl. 51) is 12.5 cm in height and has a circumference of 42 cm in the middle. The diameter of its mouth is 8.5 cm while the base has a diameter of 9.5 cm. Another water-vessel is channel-spouted and has its lid also (Pl. 52). It is, however, broken into pieces. Another channel-spouted *loṭā* has survived only in part. An *arghyā* (Pl. 53) and a decorated conch shell (Pl. 54), which must have been used in worship and rituals, too, have been recovered in the hoard.

Nimbate figures of Ambikā (Pl. 55), Dharaṇendra, a male figure seated in *sukhāsana* holding a *vīja-puraka* in the right hand (Pl. 56), a standing male figure holding a staff (Pl. 57) and a female fly-whisker (Pl. 58), which all seem to have detached from the images, complete our list of the Jaina images.

B. BUDDHIST IMAGES

As noted above, the Hansi hoard contains two Buddhist images also. One of these shows Buddha in the *bhūmisparśa-mudrā,* symbolizing the Great Enlightenment of the Śākya prince under the Bodhi tree at Bodh-Gayā (Pl. 59). Seated straight in *vajra-paryaṅkāsana* on the pericarp of an ovalish lotus with the left hand placed on the lap with palm upward and the right one resting against his right knee and pointing downwards, he looks to be a calm and serene figure. The pedestal below the lotus is completely gone. The bronze is badly mutilated and corroded concealing the details. The hair with schematic curls and the topknot may still be made out. The oval face is badly rubbed off and a part of it below the nose has gone off leaving a depression. The plump cheeks and eyes with drooping lids and thick eyebrows, however, may still be discerned. There was probably an *ūrṇā* also on the forehead. The extant left earlobe hangs down almost touching the left shoulder. A thick line across the chest running from over the left shoulder to the right armpit indicates the diaphanous *uttarāsaṅga*. The figure was probably clad in an *antarvāsa* also, as there are faint traces of its portion spread

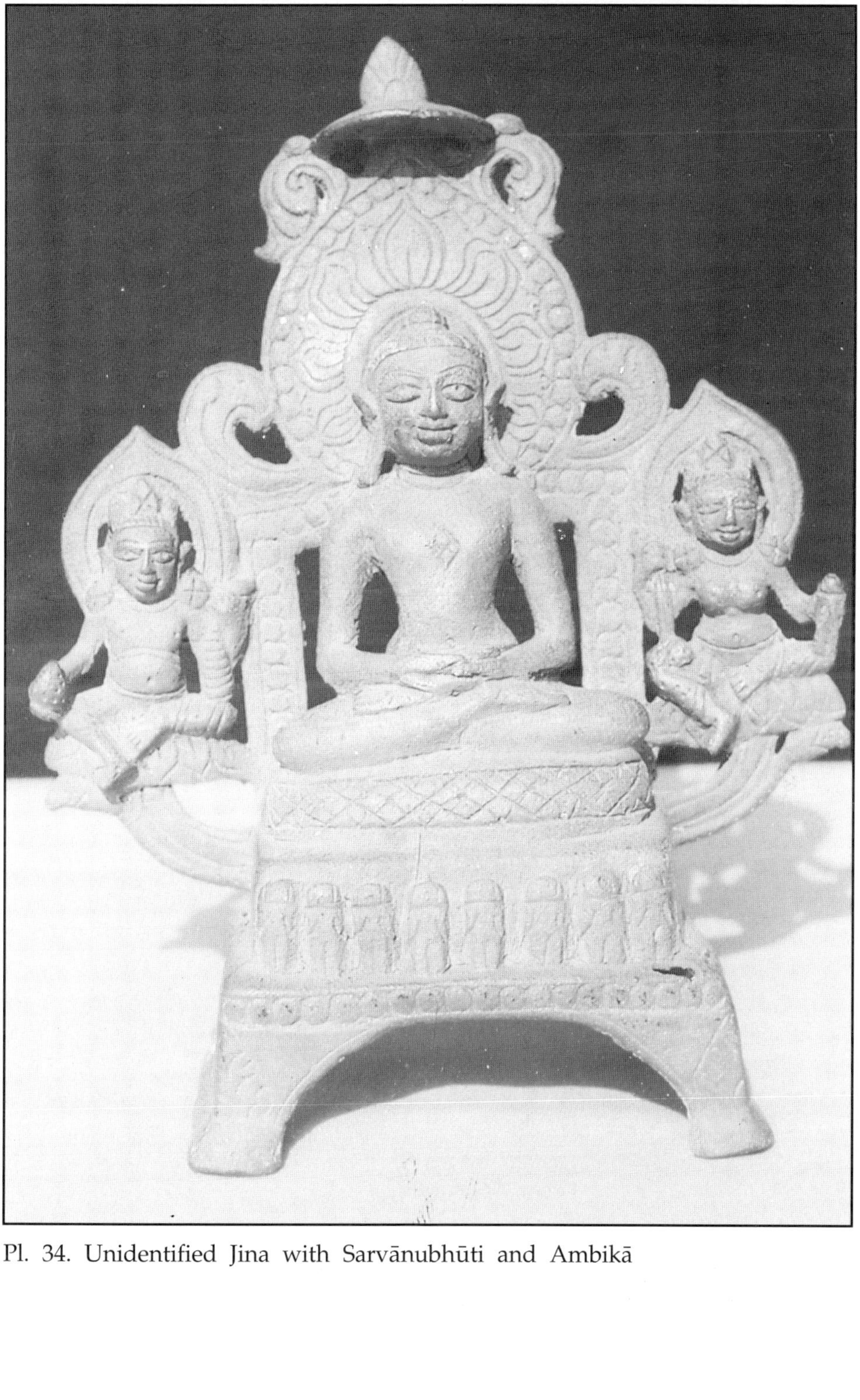

Pl. 34. Unidentified Jina with Sarvānubhūti and Ambikā

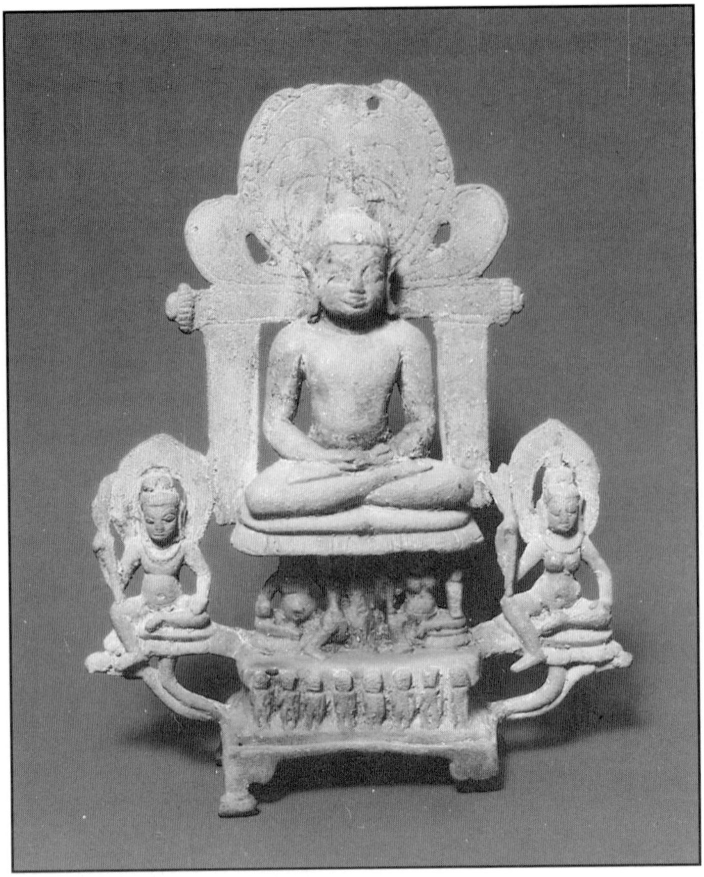

Pl. 35a. Unidentified tīrthaṅkara

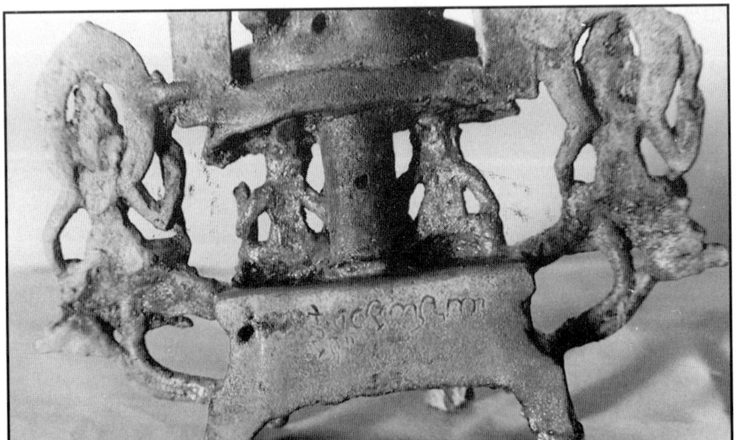

Pl. 35b. Inscription at the back

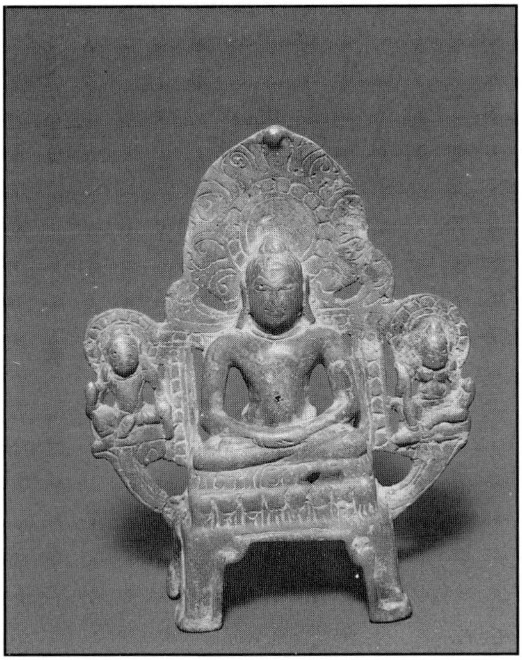

Pl. 36

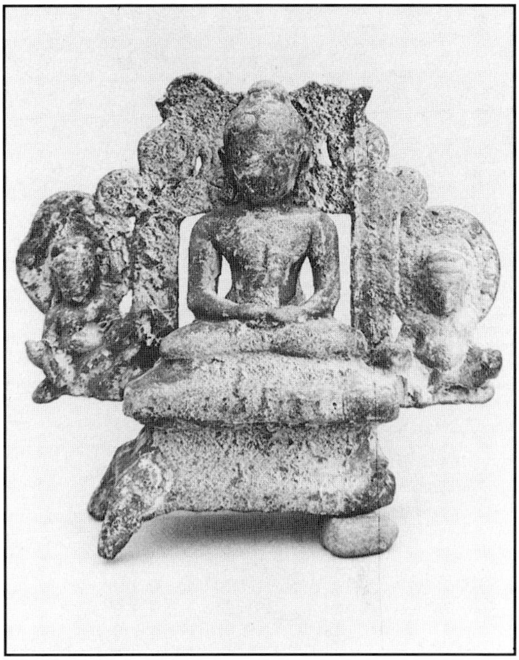

Pl. 37

Pls. 36-37. Unidentified Jinas

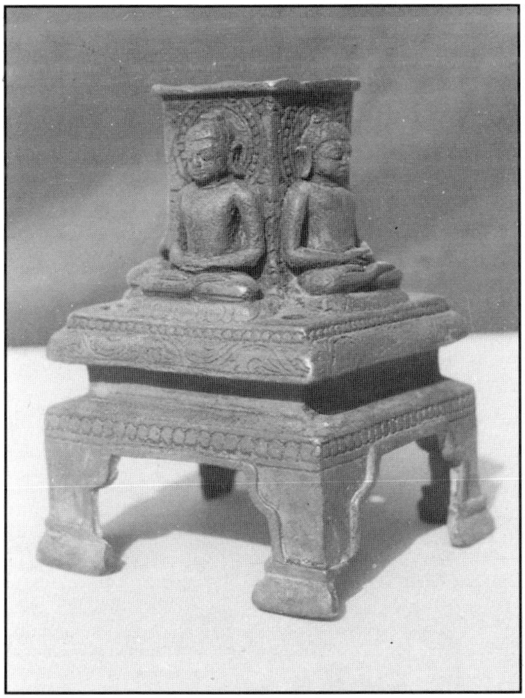

Pl. 38a. Sarvatobhadrikā

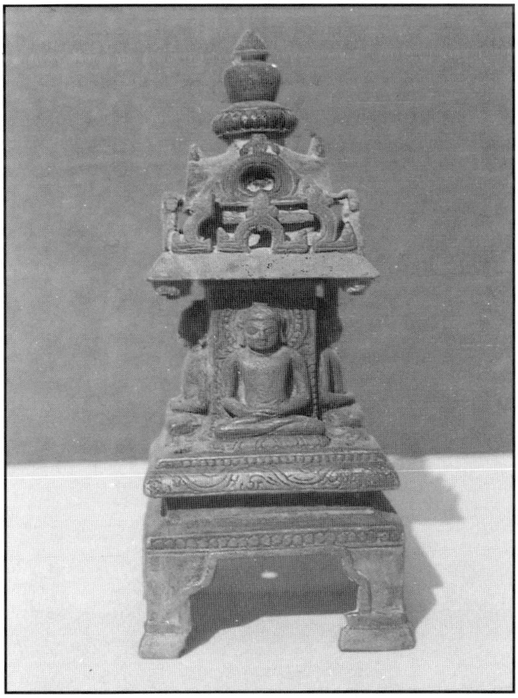

Pl. 38b. Sarvatobhadrikā with the upper part

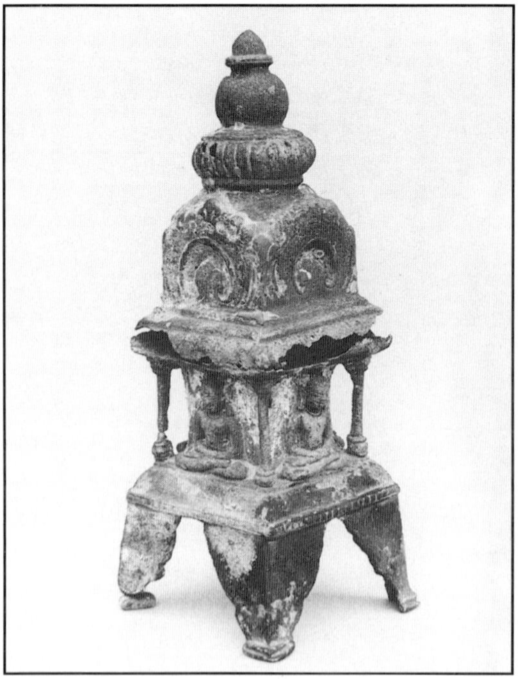

Pl. 39. Sarvatobhadikā with its upper part

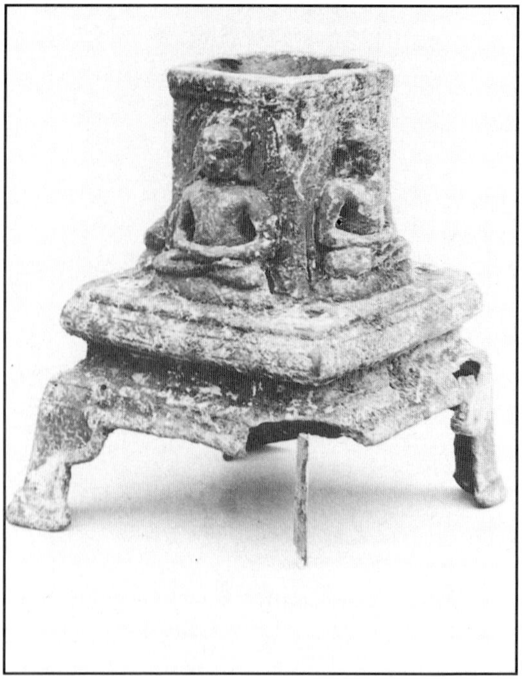

Pl. 40. Sarvatobhadrikā

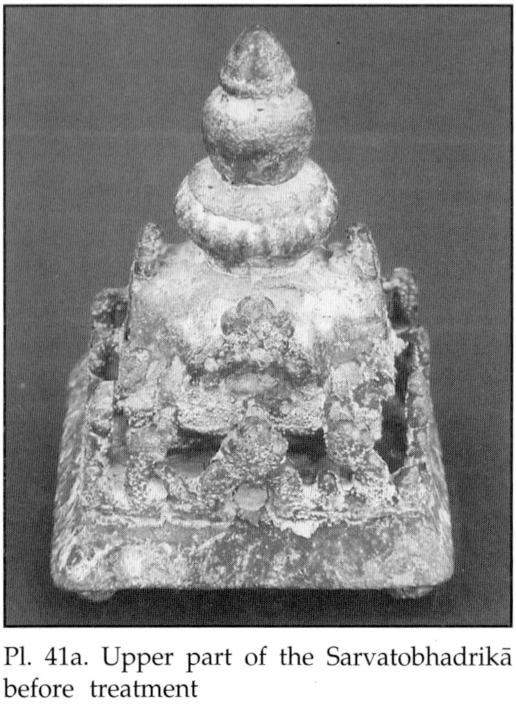

Pl. 41a. Upper part of the Sarvatobhadrikā before treatment

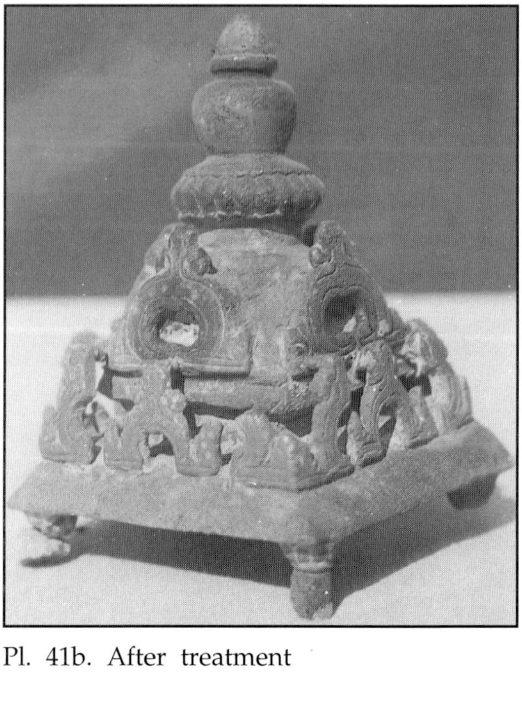

Pl. 41b. After treatment

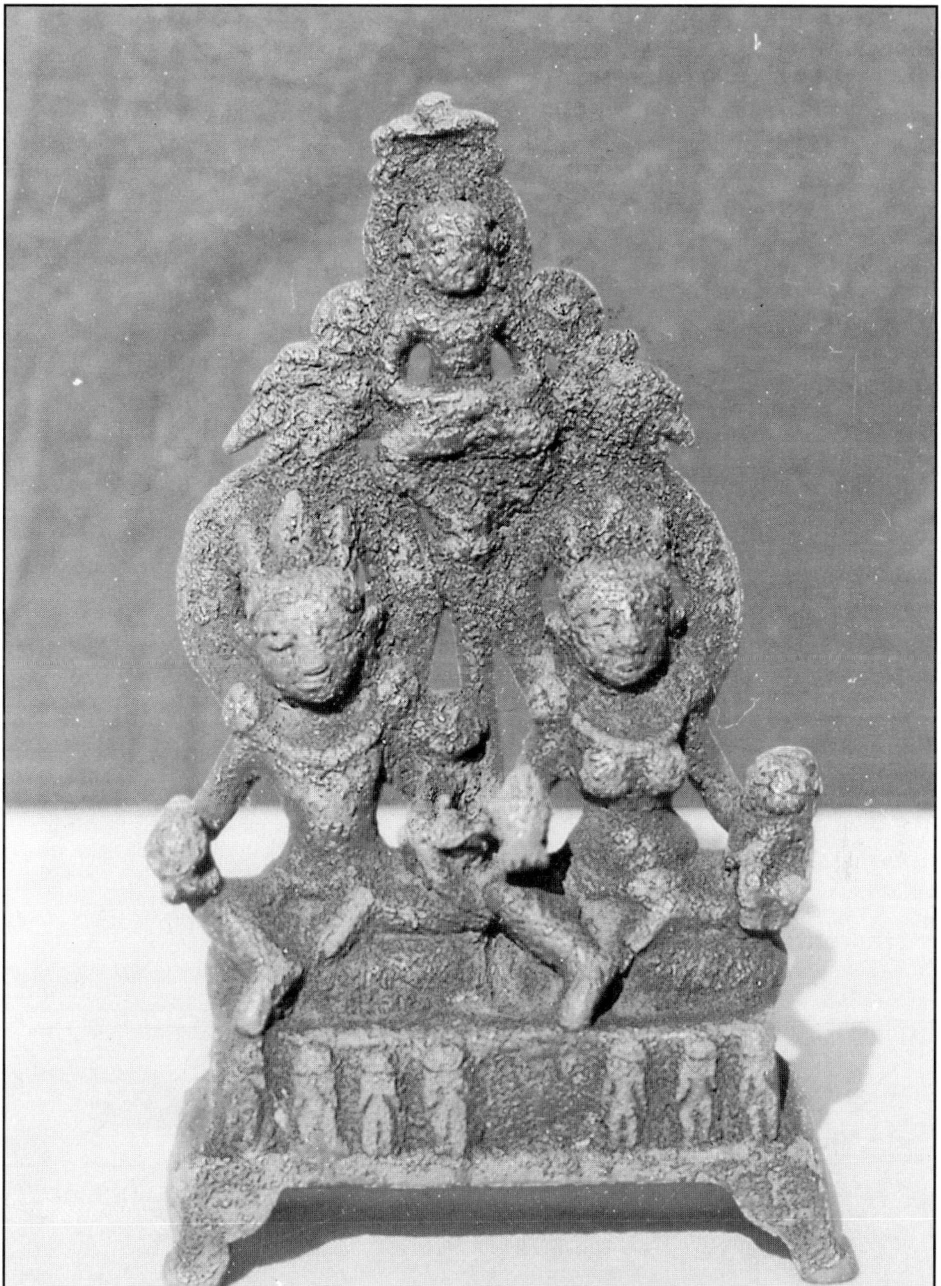

Pl. 42. Parents of the Jina

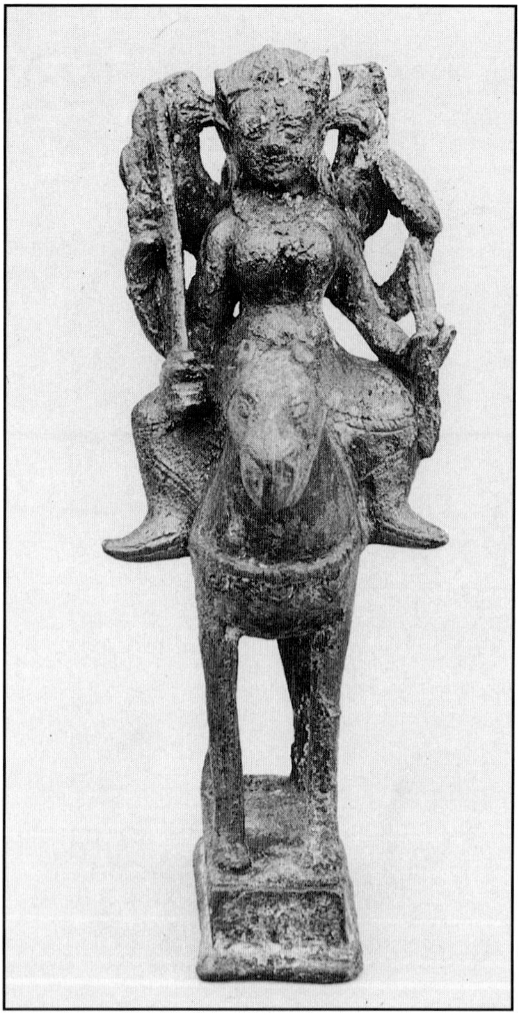

Pl. 43a. Achchhuptā, front view

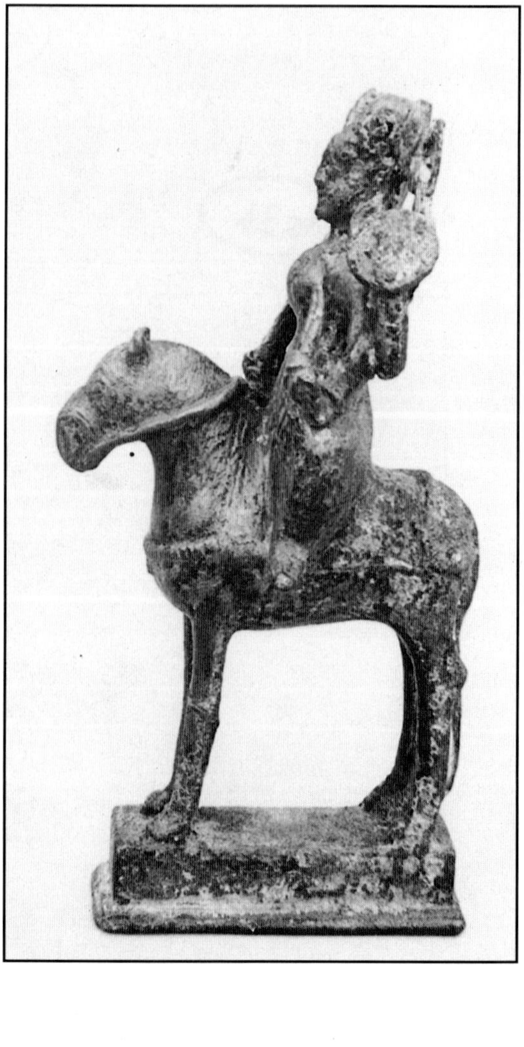

Pl. 43b. Side view

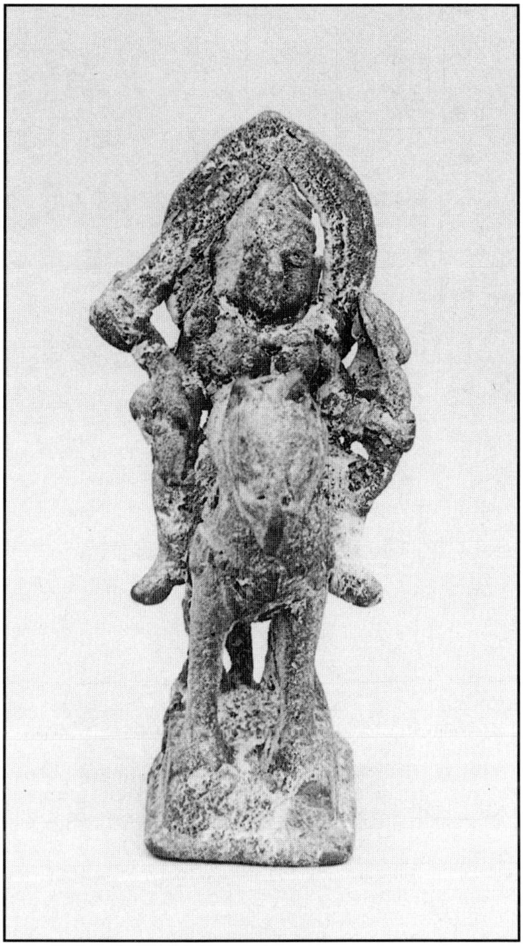

Pl. 44a. Achchhuptā, front view

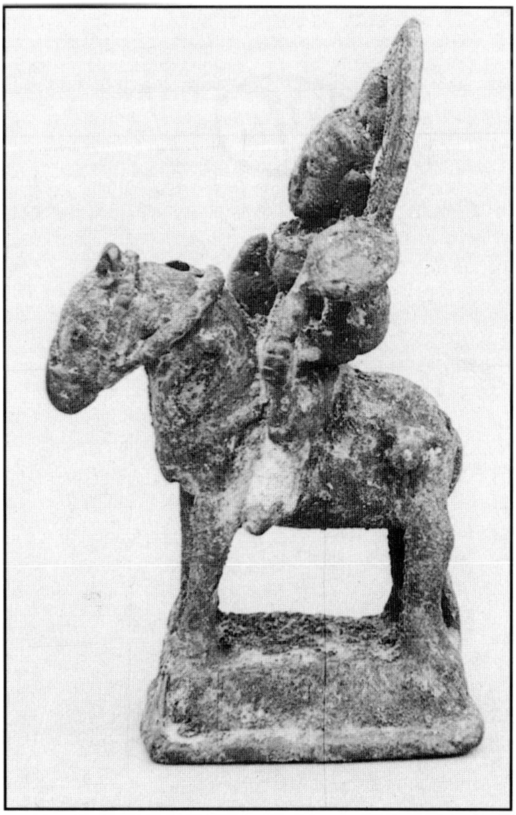

Pl. 44b. Side view

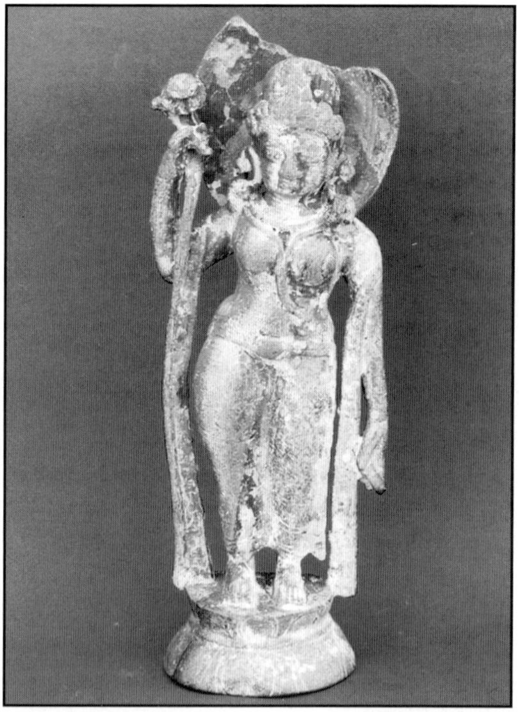

Pl. 45

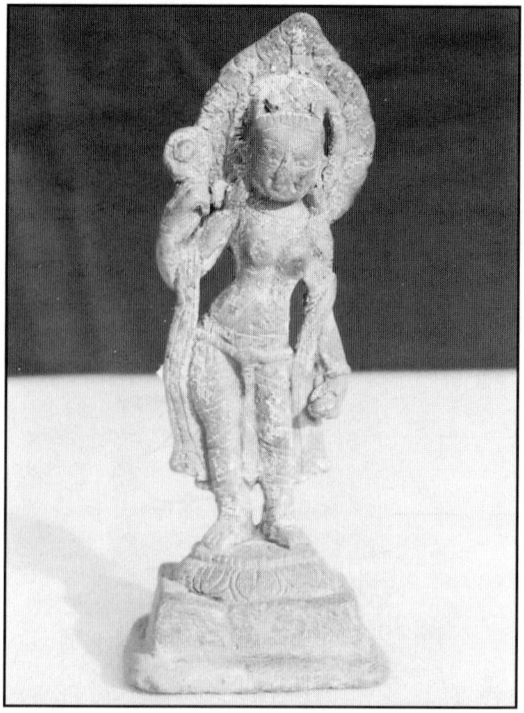

Pl. 46

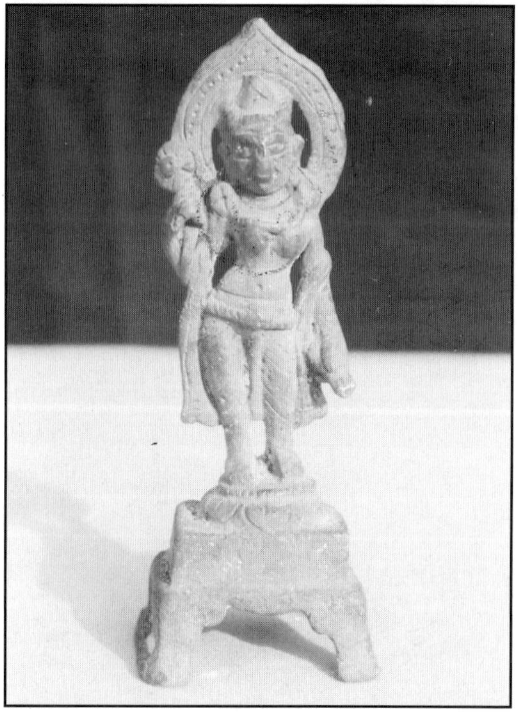

Pl. 47

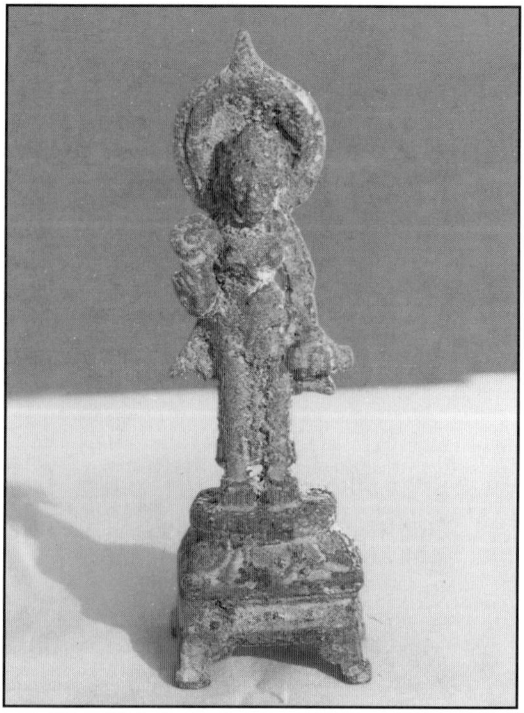

Pl. 48

Pls. 45-48. Sarasvatī

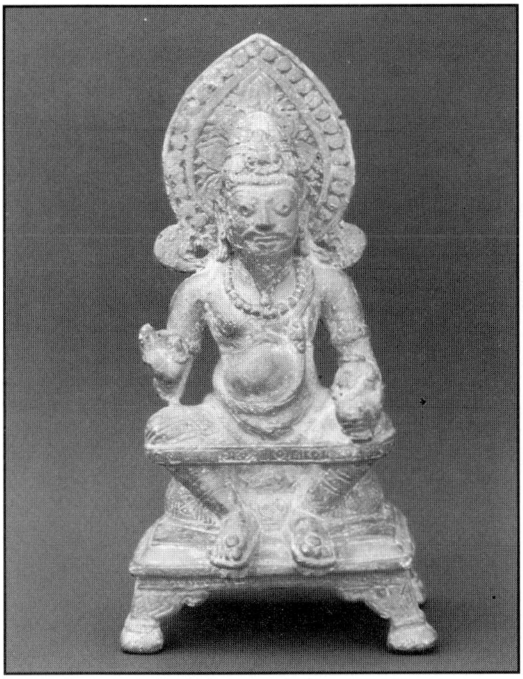

Pl. 49. Jaina Āchārya (?)

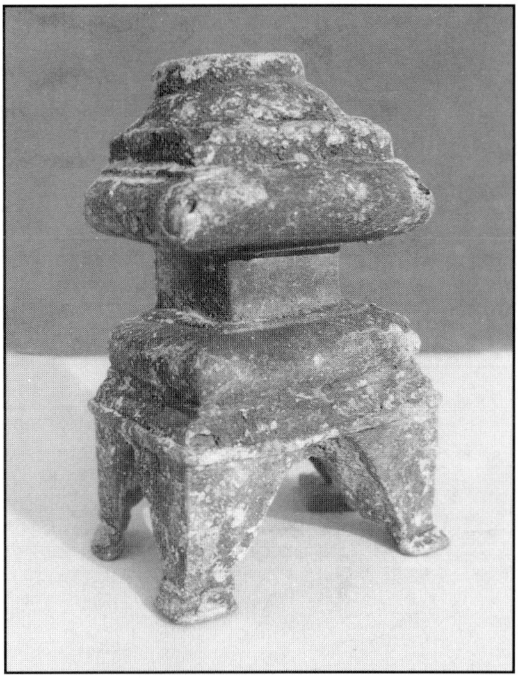

Pl. 50. *Pīṭhikā*

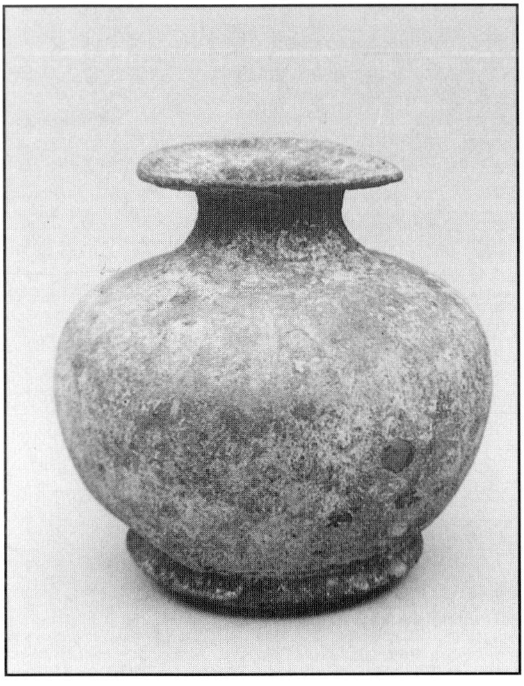

Pl. 51. Water-pot (*Loṭā*)

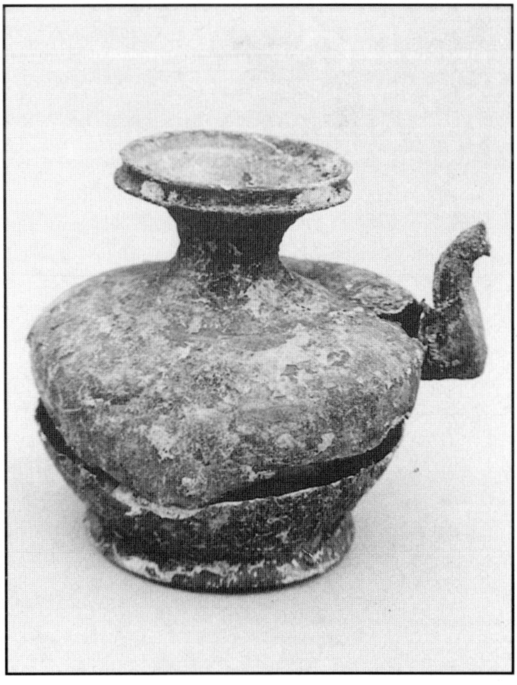

Pl. 52. Channel-spouted water-pot

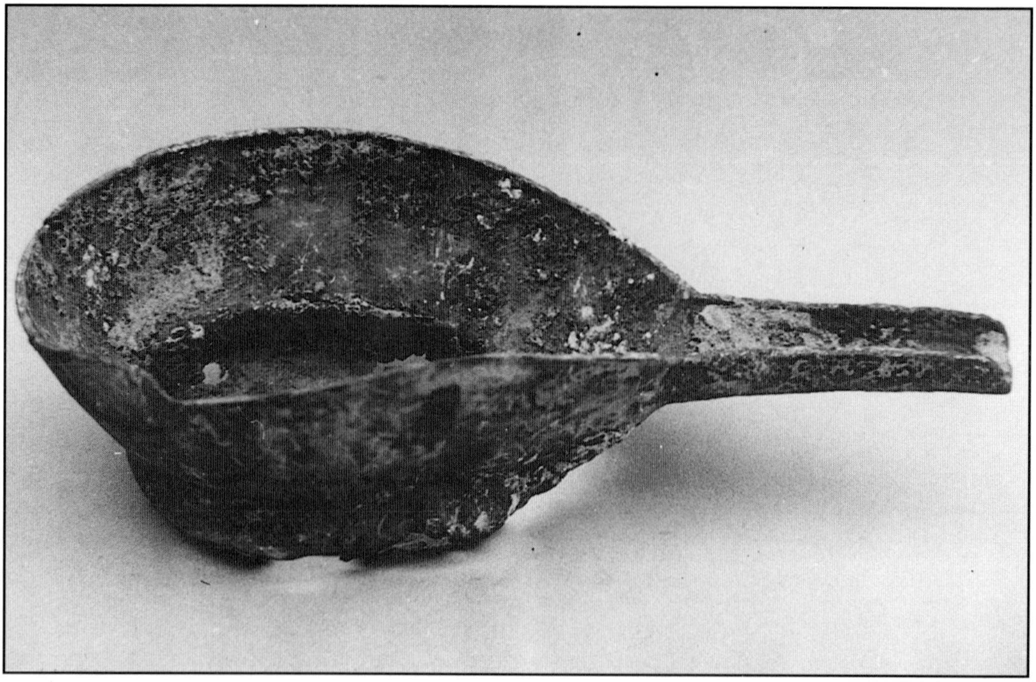

Pl. 53. Ladle (*arghyā*)

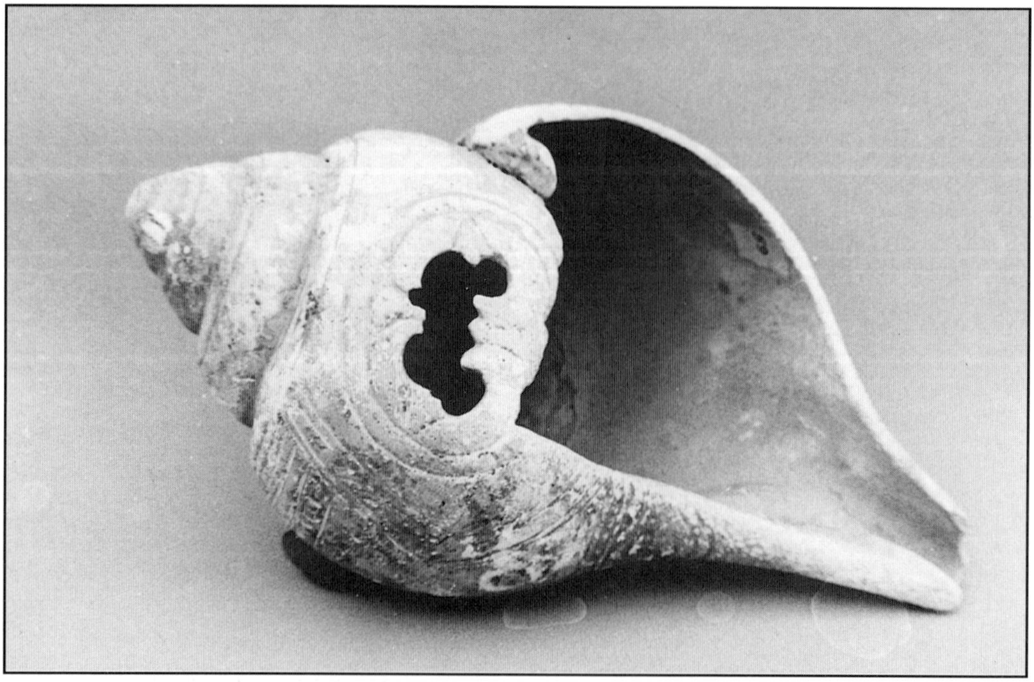

Pl. 54. Engraved conch (*Śaṅkha*)

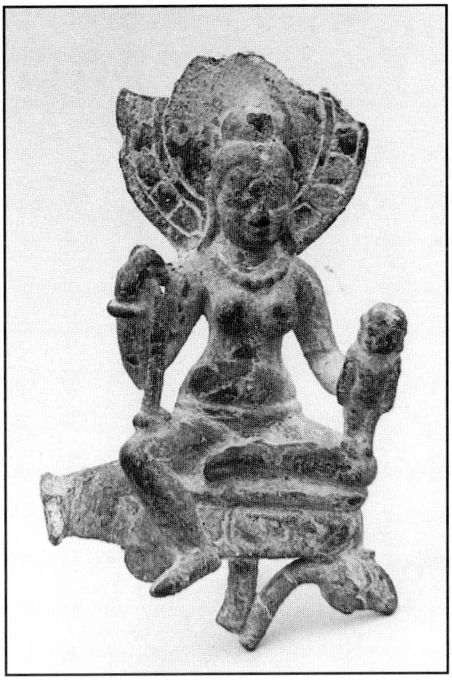

Pl. 55. Detached figure of Ambikā

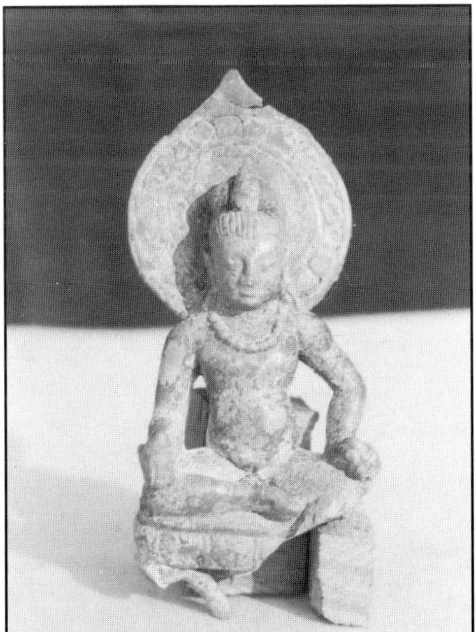

Pl. 56. Detached male figure

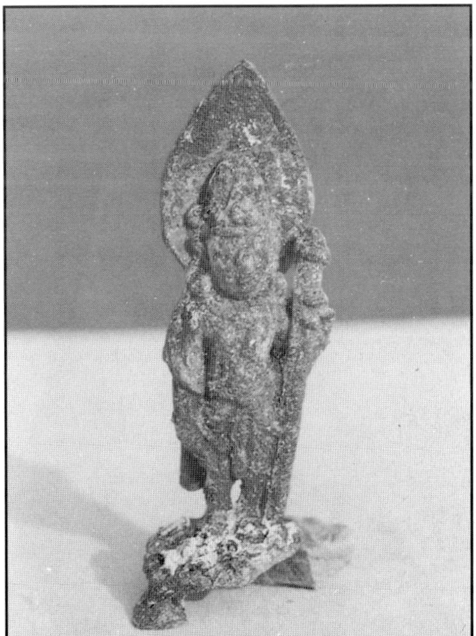

Pl. 57. Detached *daṇḍa-dhara* (*dvārapāla*)

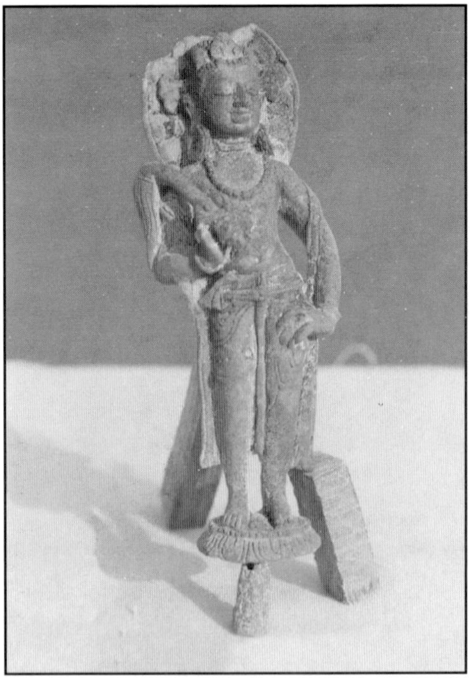

Pl. 58. Detached figure of a female fly-whisker

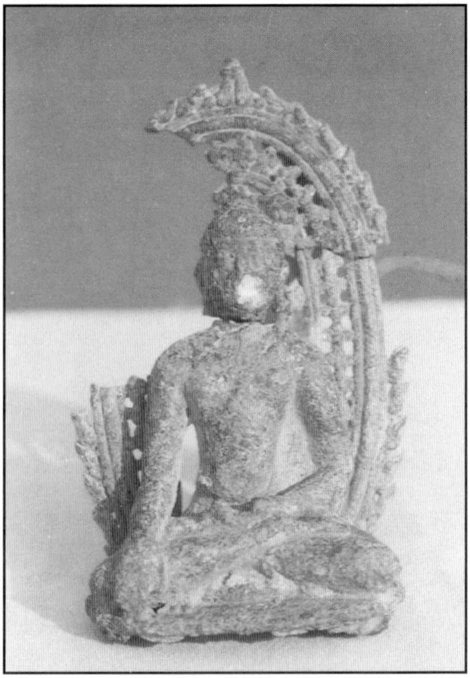

Pl. 59. Buddha in *bhūmisparśa-mudrā*

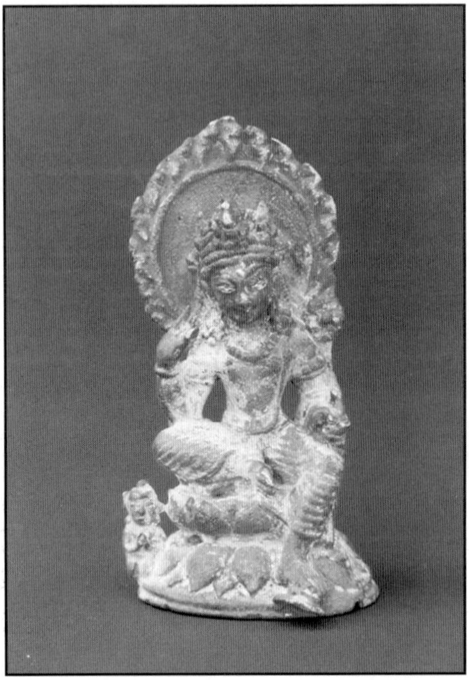

Pl. 60a. Avalokiteśvara Padmapāṇi

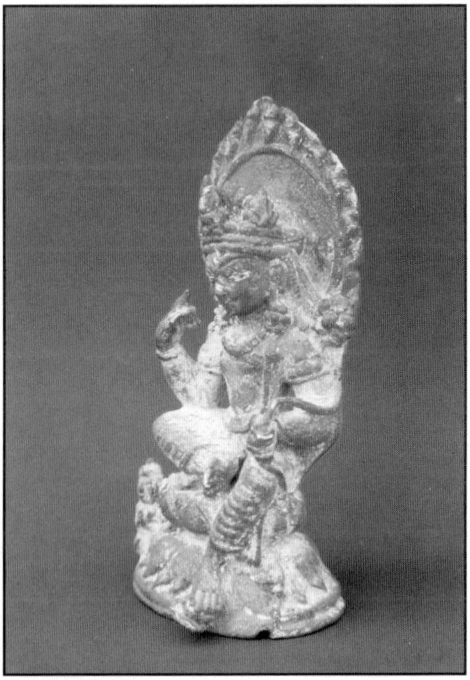

Pl. 60b. Side view

on the seat. At the back is a big horseshoe-shaped halo, broken on the proper right hand side. A part of the edge on the other side is also lost. The halo consists of three plain mouldings enclosed within a border bedecked with a continuous row of flames. Between these three plain mouldings and probably another set of similar mouldings there is four-dot lotus decoration. The apex is crowned with an indistinct projecting finial.

Like all other bronzes of the Hansi hoard, it is a small, light and easily portable image. Evidently, the icon was under prolonged religious use and underwent repeated applications of sandal paste and the like. Presented in full frontality, as most of the images of this type are, it is not accompanied by any Bodhisattvas, attendants or devotees. The oval serene face, broad chest with round shoulders, long arms and tall body, attenuated waist and sensitively modelled limbs, the beautifully bedecked long elliptical halo covering the whole of the back portion and rising above the head bestow this figure a distinctive grace. When complete and fresh, it must have been a masterpiece.

The thick folds of drapery across the chest may be compared with that of the bronze Buddha from Amaravati dated to *circa* sixth century AD.[15] The long elliptical halo simulates the one as seen in a bronze image from Achutrajpur[16] and Kurkihar,[17] datable to a period from eighth to tenth centuries AD. The absence of any inscription and badly rubbed off face make it slightly difficult to date this image very precisely. However, on the basis of fairly good modelling, simplicity of composition and stylistic consideration, it may be attributed to *circa* eighth century AD.

It may be noted that Buddhist images are not as abundant in western and northern India, particularly north of Delhi, as in eastern India. During the early medieval period, bronze Buddhist figures are still more rare.

The second figure represents Avalokiteśvara Padmapāṇī (Pl. 60a) seated beautifully in *lalitāsana* on the pericarp of a finely executed *viśva-padma* having two rows of petals. His right leg is folded and the left hangs down with foot placed on a roundish footrest attached to the bottom of the lotus-pedestal. The folds of the *antarīya* have been carved with care and grace. The Lokeśvara wears a beaded crown with three ornate triangular projections, the central one of which bears a tiny seated image of Amitābha in *dhyāna-mudrā* 'meditative posture'. The eyes and the circular mark on the forehead are inlaid with silver.

Several coiled locks of hair may be seen falling gracefully on the shoulders. The Bodhisattva bears ear ornaments of a cluster of round flowers and has auspicious lines around the neck. He wears an *ekāvalī* of big pearls, the sacred thread, beaded armlets and *valayas*. He holds a lotus by its long stalk in his left hand, placed on the corresponding thigh. The right hand is disposed in a peculiar pose raised to the level of the shoulder with palm inwards and thumb and the middle finger bent, probably to touch each other (Pl. 60b). Though not exactly similar yet it is nearer to the *chin-mudrā*, which too is rare in the images of Avalokiteśvara Padmapāṇi. The facial expression, however, betrays pensive mood. There is a circular halo with flamboyant edge behind the head and a small figure of a devotee with folded hands has been attached to the pedestal to the right of the Bodhisattva.

Eyes gilded with silver look like wide-open eyes but this is only the effect of gilding. Quasi-closed eyes are almost a ubiquitous feature of such figures. The face is placid. The face and the sturdy bust look somewhat heavy in comparison to other limbs of the body. The image is covered with thick coats of sandal paste indicating long period of worship. Being better preserved, however, it shows sharp features. The modelling appears to have been fairly good. On an overall consideration, this small icon measuring 11.0 X 5.5 cm may be attributed to the early eighth century AD.

Bronze images were quite popular in eastern and western India, even in Kashmir and Himachal Pradesh, during the early medieval period but few specimens are known from the Punjab-Haryana region. And hence their importance.

NOTES AND REFERENCES

1. For details, see U.P. Shah, *Jaina Rūpa-Maṇḍana*, Vol. I, New Delhi, 1987, pp. 115ff.
2. *Ibid.*, pp. 159-60.
3. *Ibid.*, Pls. 103-4.
4. *Nāyādhammakahāo* (edited by N.V. Vaidya), Poona, 1940, p. 95.
5. Shah (1987), *op. cit.*, p. 129. See also *Lalit-Kala*, Nos. 1-2, Pl. XI, Pl. 5.
6. Umakant P. Shah, *Akota Bronzes*, Bombay, 1959, Pls. 17 b, 26 a & b, 29 b, 30 b, 31 b, 32 a & c, etc.
7. *Ibid.*, Pls. 17 b, 22, 25, 26 a & b, 27 a & b, 28, etc.
8. *Ibid.*, p. 39, Pl. 29 b.

9. *Ibid.*, Pls. 22, 25, 49, 55 and 60.

10. The epigraph may alternatively be translated as "(This image was) caused to be made by Vallasukhā Devī, wife of Chandra."

11. Similar depiction of Brahmā may be seen on the pedestals of bronze images of Pārśvanātha found from Gaurau in district Nagaur in Rajasthan. For details, see, Harphool Singh, "Gaurau kī aprakāśita dhātu pratimāeṃ", *The Researcher*, Jaipur, Vol. XVI-XVII (1995-96), pp. 61-65, Pls. XXV-XXVIII. See also *The Great Tradition: Indian Bronze Masterpieces*, Festival of India, New Delhi, 1988, Fig. 12-13.

12. Such folds can be seen in other Jaina images also. See *Akota Bronzes*, Pls. 11, 25, 27 a, 28, 29 a & b, 30 a, etc.

13. *Ibid.*, pp. 36-37, Pl. 24.

14. *Ibid.*, Pls. 18, 19, 33 and 37.

15. D.R. Thapar, *Icons in Bronze*, Bombay, 1961, Pl. XXIV. A.

16. Debala Mitra, *Bronzes from Achutrajpur, Orissa*, Delhi, 1978, Pls. 31, 38-40, 42, 44, 47, etc.

17. Thapar, *op. cit.*, Pls. XXVIII and XXXI.

III

Epilogue

We have seen above that the Hansi hoard presents a rich variety of Jaina images. Pārśvanātha was the most popular tīrthaṅkara at Hansi. Though he is always shown under the canopy of seven-hooded cobra and bull and crescent are shown as the cognizances of Ṛishabhanātha and Chandraprabha, yet the cognizances of all the tīrthaṅkaras have not been shown in the images of this hoard. Ādinātha (Pl. 4), in one instance shows a *chakra* with two outward moving lions on the pedestal. Some other Jina figures also show similar pedestals. Yaksha Sarvānubhūti and yakshī Ambikā have been shown accompanying Pārśva and other Jinas. So these images represent the stage when neither the cognizances were an essential adjunct of the Jinas nor their yakshas and yakshīs were shown with them essentially. No specimen shows the vehicle of Sarvānubhūti and Ambikā. Most of the images depict only eight figures of the planetary divinities as we see in the western bronzes also. They bear a close resemblance to Akota bronzes. The depiction of Brahmā on the pedestals of some of the images of Pārśvanātha has a parallel in some images of this tīrthaṅkara found from the village Gaurau in district Nagaur of Rajasthan. The artists of Hansi thus seem to have been influenced by the art activities of Rajasthan and Gujarat. Stylistically most of the bronzes in the hoard may be assigned to *circa* eighth century AD and this date is corroborated by the palaeographic evidence of the inscriptions found engraved on some of the images. Many images have retained a coating of the sandal paste indicating that they had been under worship before they were buried probably at the time of Masud's invasion of Hansi in AD 1037.

These images belong to both the sects of the Jainas, i.e. the Śvetāmbaras and the Digambaras, and furnish very significant evidence of the harmony which existed between these sects at Hansi during the early medieval period.

Masud put to sword men, women and children of Hansi indiscriminately, took away enormous spoils and women to Ghazni who were later sold as slaves there. He appointed his son Majdud to govern Hansi and marched therefrom towards Sonepat whose governor Rai Dipal Hara fled away making Masud's task easy. When he returned to Ghazni, he found that his expedition to Hansi was a real blunder as in his absence the Saljuqs had plundered Talgana and Fariyab, two important towns of his dominion. Taking advantage of the dissentions in the Ghaznavid empire, Kumārapāla Tomara of Delhi, who had earlier lost the war against Masud, captured Hansi and Thanesar in AD 1043.[1] The Turks attacked Hansi again after more than a century in AD 1151-52 when it was ruled over by Tomara Madanapāla. Bahram, who led the Turks, was vanquished as the Chauhan Vigraharāja also helped Madanapāla.[2] Vigraharāja, however, defeated the Tomaras in VS 1209 (= AD 1152) and occupied Hansi and other towns.[3] Bahram's successor Khusro also led a futile expedition to capture Hansi in AD 1166.[4] The Hansi inscription of Pṛithvīrāja II (VS 1224) informs that his maternal uncle Kilhaṇa was appointed the governor of Hansi.[6] *Kharatara-gachchha-bṛihad-gurvāvali*[7] tells us that when the Jaina teacher Jinapāla visited Hansi in VS 1228 (= AD 1171), it was governed by Bhīma Siṃha who accorded a grand reception to the Āchārya. Bhīma Siṃha also arranged a dialogue between Jinapati Sūri and a Digambara scholar of the town. In VS 1221, Nāgadatta was placed on the post of Vāchanāchārya at Āsikā. In VS 1238 (= AD 1181), two great Jinas (*bṛihajjinayugala*) were installed at Hansi.[8] This indicates that the restoration and construction of the shrines which had been destroyed earlier had been taking place at Hansi during this period. The *Gurvāvali* tells us that Jineśvara Sūri had made Hansi his permanent abode. In the great *maṭha* 'establishment' with a rich library, he used to teach the sons of laymen (*śrāvaka-putras*). Hansi became a great centre of Jainism under him. One of his pupils Jinavallabha Sūri became a great scholar and propagator of Jainism in the region. The *Gurvāvali* contains an account of the Jaina Āchāryas from Varddhamāna to Jinaprabha (from eleventh to fourteenth century AD) and throws welcome light on the state and propagation of Jainism at Hansi and the surrounding regions.[9] Jainism is still a living religion at Hansi.

We thus see that the hoard of bronzes from Hansi throws welcome light on the state of Jainism and Jaina art at Hansi during the eighth through tenth centuries and the *Kharatara-gachchha-bṛihad-gurvāvalī* throws further light on Jainism and the activities of the Jaina monks in the area during the eleventh through the thirteenth centuries AD.

The two images of Buddha and Avalokiteśvara with traces of sandal paste buried along with the Jaina images are also very important as they betray the continuity of the worship of Buddha and the religious tolerance and co-operation between the followers of the Jaina and Buddhist faiths up to AD 1037 when the hoard was buried.

Metal images belonging to the medieval period are well known from eastern and western India as well as from Kashmir and Himachal Pradesh but none have ever been found from the Punjab-Haryana region. This hoard furnishes important evidence and fills the gap and therefore its importance cannot be overstated.

NOTES AND REFERENCES

1. Muhammad Habib, *Sultan Mahmud of Ghazni*, Aligarh, 1961, pp. 81-91; Ishwari Prasad, *History of Medieval India*, Allahabad, 1933, pp. 130 ff. Also see H.N. Dvivedi, *Dillī ke Tomara* (Hindi), Gwalior, 1963, pp. 230 ff and R.C. Majumdar & A.D. Pusalkar (Eds.), *The Struggle for Empire*, Bombay, 1955, p. 94.
2. Dvivedi, *op. cit.*, pp. 253ff.
3. *Epigraphia Indica*, XXVI, p. 150.
4. Dvivedi, *loc. cit.*
5. D.R. Bhandarkar, "Hansi Stone Inscription of Pṛithvīrāja (Vikama) Samvat 1224", *Indian Antiquary*, Vol. XLI (1912), vv. 3-5.
6. Acharya Jina Vijaya Muni (Ed.), *Kharataragachchha-bṛihadgurvāvali*, Bombay, 1956, p. 23.
7. *Ibid.*, pp. 20, 80.
8. *Ibid.*, pp. 8ff.

Bibliography

Afif, Shams Siraj, *Tarikh-i-Firuzshahi*, Calcutta, 1890.

Agrawala, R.C., "Celts From Hansi, Haryana", *Kusumañjali — New Interpretation of Indian Art & Culture: Sh. C. Sivaramamurti Commemoration Volume*, edited by M.S. Nagaraja Rao, Vol. I, Delhi, 1987.

Ahluwalia, M.S., "Medieval Hansi", *Proceedings of the Punjab History Congress, Sixth Session*, Patiala (March 19-20, 1971), pp. 95-103.

Allan, John, *Catalogue of the Coins of Ancient India*, London, 1936 (Indian Reprint, Delhi, 1975).

Aṇuyogadvāra Sūtra, Bombay, 1921.

Aṇuyogadvāra Chūrṇī with Vṛitti, Ratlam, 1928.

Annual Report of the Archaeological Survey of India 1922-23.

Beal, Samuel, *Buddhist Records of the Western World*, London, 1884, I.

——, *Life of Hiuen-Tsiang by Hwui-Li*, London, 1882.

Bhagwan Deva, Acharya, *Vīra-bhūmi Hariyānā* (Hindi), Jhajjar, 1965.

Bhandarkar, D.R., "Hansi Stone Inscription of Pṛithvīrāja (Vikama) Samvat 1224", *Indian Antiquary*, Vol. XLI (1912), vv. 3-5.

Bharadwaj, O.P., *Studies in the Historical Geography of Ancient India*, Delhi, 1986.

Bidwel, Shelford, *Swords for Hire*, London, 1971.

Chhabra, B.Ch., "Aśokan Pillar At Hissar, Panjab", *Vishveshvaranand Indological Journal*, Vol. II, Pt. ii (Sept. 1964).

Divyāvadāna (ed. by Cowell and Neil).

Cunningham, Alexander, *Archaeological Survey of India, Report for the Year 1872-73*, Vol. V (Reprint, Varanasi, 1966).

——, *Ancient Geography of India* (Reprint, Varanasi, 1963).

Dasgupta, K.K., *Tribal History of Ancient India — A Numismatic Approach*, Calcutta, 1974.

Deshpande, M.N., "The Background and Tradition", in *Jaina Art and Architecture*, edited by A. Ghosh, Vol. I, New Delhi, 1974.

Dvivedi, H.N., *Dillī ke Tomara* (Hindi), Gwalior, 1963.

Elliot, H.M. and Dowson, J., *History of India as told by its own Historians*, Vol. II.

Fabri, Charles. "Archaeology in the Punjab", *Marg*, X (2), March 1957.

Fausboll, V., *The Jataka*, London, 1963, Vol. VI.

Franklin, W., *The Military Memoirs of George Thomas*, London, 1803.

Garrick, H.B.W., *Archaeological Survey Report*, Vol. XXIII.

Gazetteer of Hissar District, Lahore, 1883-84.

Grey, C., *European Adventurers of Northern India (1785-1849)*, edited by H.L.O. Garret, Lahore, 1929.

Gupta, S.P., *The Indus-Sarasvati Civilization*, Delhi, 1996.

Habib, Muhammad, *Sultan Mahmud of Ghazni*, Aligarh, 1961.

Handa, Devendra, *Heritage of Haryana: Buddhist Remains*, Chandigarh, 1989.

——, "Varāha Images from Haryana", in *Researches in Indian History, Archaeology, Art and Religion (Prof. Upendra Thakur Felicitation Volume)*, edited by G. Kuppuram and K. Kumudmani, Vol. I, Delhi, 1990.

——, "Two Buddhist Bronzes from Hansi", in *Buddhist Art and Thought*, edited by K.K. Mittal & Ashvini Agrawal, New Delhi, 1993.

——, "Mahishasuramardini in the Medieval Art of Haryana", in *Researches in Indian Archaeology, Art, Architecture, Culture and Religion (Vijaya Kanta Mishra Commemoration Volume)*, ed. by P.K. Mishra, Delhi, 1995, Vol. II.

——, "Jaina Bronze Hoard from Hansi — A Preliminary Study", in *The Bounteous Tree: Treasures in Indian Art and Culture*, edited by K.K. Chakravarty, Vol. II, Delhi, 1997, pp. 293-302 and *Roopa-Lekhā*, Vol. LXVII-LXXI, March 2001, pp. 1-13.

Hultzsch, E., "Delhi-Topra Pillar Edicts", *Corpus Inscriptionum Indicarum*, Vol. I, London, 1925.

Imperial Gazetteer of India, Vol. I.

Indian Archaeology 1963-64 — A Review.

Jain, Jyoti Prasad, *The Jaina Sources of the History of Ancient India*, Delhi, 1964.

Jana Sāhitya, Patiala, Vol. IV, Nos. 10-11.

Journal of the Royal Asiatic Society of Bengal, Vol. VII.

Kāntisāgara, Muni, *Khaṇḍaharoṃ kā Vaibhava* (Hindi), 2nd ed., Banaras, 1959.

Khatri, J.S. and Acharya, M., "Kunal — A New Indus-Sarasvati Site", *Purātattva*, No. 25.

Lalit-Kala, Nos. 1-2 (1955-56).

Lohan, Aditya, *A Historico-Cultural Study of the Hansi Region (From The Earliest Times To A.D. 1526)*, Ph. D. Thesis (Unpublished), Kurukshetra University, Kurukshetra, 1988.

Majumdar, R.C. and Pusalkar, A.D. (Eds.), *The Struggle for Empire*, Bombay, 1955.

Marshall, John, *Taxila*, 3 Vols., Cambridge, 1951.

——, *Guide to Taxila*, Cambridge, 1960.

McCrindle, J.W., *Ancient India as Described by Megasthenes and Arrian*, Revised 2nd ed., Calcutta, 1960.

Mitra, Debala, *Bronzes from Achutrajpur, Orissa*, Delhi, 1978.

Müeller, Max (Gen. Ed.), *Sacred Books of the East*, Vol. XVII.

Muni, Acharya Jina Vijaya (Ed.), *Kharataragachchha-bṛihadgurvāvali*, Bombay, 1956.

Nagarāja, Muni-Śrī, *Mahāvīra aura Buddha kī samasāmayikatā* (Hindi), Delhi, 1971.

Nāyādhammakahāo (edited by N.V. Vaidya), Poona, 1940.

Prasad, Ishwari, *History of Medieval India*, Allahabad, 1933.

Punjab District Gazetteer: Jhelum District, Lahore, 1907.

Rajput, Bhup Singh, *Souvenir on Hansi*, August 1981.

Raverty, H.C. (Eng. Tr.), *Tabaqat-i-Nasiri* (Reprint, Delhi, 1981).

Rizvi, S.A.A., *Tughlaq Kālīna Bhārata* (Hindi), Part I, Aligarh, 1956.

Rodgers, C.J., *Revised List of Objects of Archaeological Interest in the Panjab*, Lahore, 1891.

Roy, A.K., *A History of the Jainas*, New Delhi, 1984.

Shah, Umakant P., *Akota Bronzes*, Bombay, 1959.

Shah, U.P. (Ed.), *Treasures of Jaina Bhaṇḍāras*, Ahmedabad, 1978.

——, *Jaina Rūpa-Maṇḍana*, Vol. I, New Delhi, 1987.

Singh, Harphool, "Gaurau kī aprakāśita dhātu pratimāe", *The Researcher*, Jaipur, Vol. XVI-XVII (1995-96), pp. 61-65, Pls. XXV-XXVIII.

Stein, M.A., *Archaeological Reconnaissances in North-Western India and South-Eastern Iran*, London, 1937.

Thapar, D.R., *Icons In Bronze*, Bombay, 1961.

The Great Tradition: Indian Bronze Masterpieces, Festival of India, New Delhi, 1988.

Therīgāthā, ed. N.K. Bhagwat, Bombay, 1956.

Watters, Thomas, *On Yuan Chwang's Travels in India*, Delhi, 1961, 1st Indian edition.

Yule, Paul, *Metal Work of the Bronze Age in India*, Munchen, 1985.

Index